T0193930

I Know How You Feel!

Dot Streets

authorHOUSE®

AuthorHouse™ UK
1663 Liberty Drive
Bloomington, IN 47403 USA
www.authorhouse.co.uk
Phone: 0800.197.4150

Published by AuthorHouse 11/15/2018

ISBN: 978-1-5462-9570-9 (sc)
ISBN: 978-1-5462-9569-3 (e)

Print information available on the last page.

Dedicated to my lovely husband Jim
for his constant care and support.

CONTENTS

1 Introduction   A Memoire of a Nobody ix

2 Story   My Most Extraordinary Year xv

     Chapter 1   Just One Look 1
     Chapter 2   Unexpected Help 25
     Chapter 3   The Picture....................................... 46
     Chapter 4   Overwhelmed................................... 80
     Chapter 5   Waves...115
     Chapter 6   Moving On.......................................151

3 Poetry   Rhymes and Reasons....................................159

     Section 1   How it Began...................................161
     Section 2   Therapy 168
     Section 3   The Fog..182
     Section 4   Into the Light 203

4 Information   Being an Empath 219

     My Discoveries 219
     Definition..220
     Traits of an Empath...221
     Identification...222
     Cause and Effect..223
     Both a Blessing and a Curse 225
     Coping Strategies..227
     Centring 232
     Grounding...234
     Protection...237
     Using Your Energy Wisely....................................239
     Your Special Gift..242

A Memoire

of a Nobody

Nobody

I'm nobody famous.
You won't have heard of me
In magazines or tabloids
On radio or TV
I've not been captured by the media
And I'm happy to be free
To be nobody's nobody!

Yet I'm really rather special
For there's no one just like me.
I'm a unique individual
And I think you might agree
Being special makes you somebody
And you are just like me
Because nobody is nobody.

I'd only ever associated memoires with famous people, not ordinary individuals like me. But many ordinary people have fascinating stories to tell. Mine would probably never have been written if my husband Jim had not repeatedly kept telling me years ago that I should "do something" with my poems and asking others to encourage me. I was dubious but gave Jim's idea some consideration. The more I thought about it the more I realised that it was the story behind the poems which I really wanted to tell.

It is a memoire which recounts the strangest twelve months of my life.

I was 58 years old and had recently settled happily into early retirement. With my mind no longer overwhelmed by the many forms of documentation which had become part of my role as a teacher I now felt more relaxed than I could ever remember. I have wondered if it was being so relaxed which led to the initial occurrence. But that is something I shall never know.

Catching the eye of an acquaintance is unremarkable but what happened next was a surprising start to an unprecedented year of things which I had never experienced before. My mind became overwhelmed, I was troubled by many strange happenings and for much of the time I felt I was some sort of crazy freak! It was definitely an intriguing time but I was at a loss to know how to handle many of the situations. Fortunately I would often find something to lift my spirits, raise my confidence and enable me to continue the peculiar trek for which I had been totally unprepared. Help generally came from most unexpected sources so the entire period was very unusual. It culminated in a wonderful surprise and the whole experience proved to be life-changing for me.

During the twelve months spanned by my story I delved deeply into my past, including the recall of periods of depression. I had suffered numerous bouts of varying severity over a period of about twenty years. Fortunately I eventually received appropriate long term treatment and have been free of depression since my forties.

When I looked back at the times I had succumbed to this illness I found I could recall the feelings of despair without stress. I also remembered the long and rocky road to full recovery. I have tried to portray both the depths of depression and the joy of recovery in various poems as well as writing an introduction to them which expresses my own views on depression. I hope that these may be useful to others as we are now being far more open about mental health issues.

Writing poems is not one of my hobbies. I've never attended a poetry writing course or been a member of a poetry club. I had previously had one short spell of composing verse, but this time was different, gradually intensifying until writing poems, both by night and by day, became an overwhelming compulsion the significance of which I didn't appreciate until much later. Many of my poems are in the section "Rhymes and Reasons", with a few included in my memoire.

During my bizarre year I had no understanding of what was happening to me. I sought information but the frustration of being unable to find any added to my discomfort. For much of the time it seemed I was going crazy. I felt very alone and fearful. Towards the end of those twelve months I did discover the cause of what had been happening to me. I am an empath, something I had never heard of. There wasn't much information available 10 years ago. There is much more now but it strikes me that if you are as baffled and confused as I was and have never heard of an empath, you cannot access the information you need!

So the purpose of my memoire is to help others who may have similar experiences to mine. If you identify with any of the extraordinary occurrences in my memoire then the final section is for you.

I hope you will find both the story and the poems interesting but above all I hope that any reader who can relate to my odd experiences will find this book useful.

Dot Streets 2018

My Most

Extraordinary

Year

CHAPTER 1
AUTUMN 2007

Just One Look

Shrugging into our coats my friend and I shivered as we left the warmth of the building. We headed for a nearby wall for protection from the chill wind of late autumn. Someone had had the same idea and was there already, facing the bricks as he lit his cigarette. He turned and smiled at our approach.

It has become such an antisocial habit yet smoking can create small gatherings of people who otherwise would probably not speak to each other. Forced outside smokers will join and chat whilst enjoying a cigarette, as we three did. It wasn't the first time we'd been together so he was neither stranger nor friend, just an acquaintance. I've decided to call him Mark.

At some point in the conversation I glanced up at Mark. Our eyes met, and it hit me, an instantaneous, short, low blow which had an instant effect. The feeling it triggered immediately spread throughout my body and mind and overwhelmed me. I felt dazed, and my insides were churning.

Recovery was rapid, but just those few fleeting seconds had a strong effect. A stronger and longer lasting affect than I could ever have imagined. It was the start of the most extraordinary time of my life.

I recognised what hit me - that insidious invader, depression. I had enough bouts of depression in the past to know the feelings and the effects of this menace. What I had just experienced, seemingly transferred from Mark was not the worst depression, but nevertheless, it sent me plummeting back into past illnesses. It was scary but thankfully very short-lived.

When I rose from that brief recall, anger took over. No one should have to suffer that crippling, cruel disease yet I was sure that one unwitting glance revealed a victim. I didn't know how or why I had witnessed this. Nothing like this had happened to me before. But I was left with an absolute certainty that Mark was in the early stages of a depression that would grow.

I didn't for one moment doubt my gut instincts, but it was none of my business. It was an invasion of privacy. This wasn't a relative or a close friend but someone I barely knew at all, a relative stranger.

Stubbing out my cigarette, I turned away from him and returned inside, troubled about Mark and puzzled by my insight.

Although it had only lasted for seconds, my strange reaction was just the start. I had no idea of the impact that this experience would have on me in the future.

I didn't mention it to anyone, but over the next few weeks it played on my mind. I never doubted the truth of what I had experienced. It was far too strong a feeling to dismiss.

I thought about it again and again, remembering the immediate impact of just looking at Mark. The resulting feeling was so upsetting and stark, it was not something I could dismiss. There was no way that I could explain it and certainly no way I could forget it. The more I puzzled over it, the more my concern grew.

Why had I had this insight? How could it have happened? Surely there was a purpose. I had the feeling that I was meant to do something, but had no idea what I was supposed to do. I was beginning to worry and there was no point in that. I needed to put it out of my mind.

My usual way of stopping worry and escaping stress is gardening; it has been my favourite hobby for years. I always find that working out in the fresh air takes my mind away from any stress as well as providing exercise. It is both a physical and mental workout. However, winter is not the best time of year for that. I had to think of other activities which could occupy me. Jim and I had bought an old camper van which he had gutted and refitted, a laborious labour of love! My contribution to all this work was to replace the upholstery and make new curtains. It would require a great deal of measuring and calculation just to assess the amounts of material needed. Jim and I would shop together for the fabrics. Then I would be able to get to work on the transferring the measurements, cutting, and stitching with many fittings in between! It would take some time to complete.

And since my retirement I had two new hobbies. I had joined an art club at the local church and was enjoying learning about the different media and techniques. I also joined a singing company, which was how I met Mark. I had plenty to keep me occupied. I could always work on my latest painting or learn part of song for the next concert.

I saw Mark occasionally at singing rehearsals. He wasn't from my area, so I never knew when I would see him. But at some point we'd be back in smokers' corner. One friend always referred to it as the naughty corner! None of us were good advertisements for singing!

When I next saw Mark there was no repetition of my strange experience in October. But I could not get over those seconds of deep insight. I never doubted the truth of what I'd experienced and now I also sensed that my intuition was not harmful. That also seemed odd since I clearly felt that Mark's health was in harm's way. Presumably it must be that it wouldn't harm me.

I had no intention of telling Mark of my strange intuition or mentioning anything about depression. I didn't know him well enough to speak of something so personal. It would be disconcerting for him and embarrassing for me since it was such an odd thing for me to feel.

However, in the middle of one conversation which had begun quite normally, something took over me. I began saying things which had occurred to me in the previous weeks but had never considered saying and weren't connected to our current conversation. I heard myself telling him how I thought he felt about his future business trip. It would take him away for some time and arrangements had not been going well, necessitating various changes which were frustrating him.

Suddenly I found myself saying, "You don't want to go, do you? You'd rather stay here."

My words clearly took him by surprise. He stepped back a few paces as if I was getting too close, but not by way of distance. He looked both amazed and sad. When he came towards me again he was looking at the floor, shaking his head. He looked up at me, a pained expression in his eyes and a tight set to his mouth. He shrugged. He seemed apprehensive and anxious. And when he spoke his voice was low. "What can I do?"

I really had no answer, so I shrugged too and just replied, "Take care."

Once again I walked away.

It seemed my thoughts about his future were correct. When he previously talked to us of his trip, he was excited. He'd be away for months and had many plans he appeared to be eager to pursue. Frustration over the time-consuming arrangements had appeared to be the only thing bothering him. Yet somehow, I realised there was more to his dissatisfaction.

It saddened me, but wasn't disturbing; it was my initial intuition which still bothered me. I truly believed in what I had felt then, and now something else had been confirmed.

I still chose not to tell anyone because I was rather embarrassed about these feelings. I just wanted them to go away. It was as if something was sometimes taking over my mind. It made me think I wasn't really in control of myself, which was uncomfortable, but I still never doubted my intuition.

I just kept busy.

Over the Christmas period we had plenty to do. I stopped thinking about Mark and didn't see him till a couple of weeks into the New Year. As before, we were outside, smoking. In the company of others, we all chatted and Mark seemed no different from his usual self except for a bloodshot eye and slight swelling. I joked that maybe someone had punched him, but he said it was due to pressure, and he hadn't been well. As it was winter and many people had been poorly, myself included, I didn't think any more of his physical health. I didn't sense anything amiss, but my instincts were still telling me that something was wrong, and I had no reason to doubt my feelings.

As we moved to go inside I stopped Mark and hand brushed the back of his jacket, because it was covered in sand from the sandstone wall he had been leaning against.

During the following weeks I thought of Mark more often. I wondered if touching him had somehow strengthened our connection because my concern for him grew. I still felt I was supposed to do something but still had no idea what. I knew he would be leaving for his trip around this time, though I did not know exactly when. I had no idea when I would see him next, but I was becoming increasingly apprehensive about how he was.

Although I could forget about him for a while, Mark seemed to be at the back of my mind permanently, ready to come to the fore at any moment. And the feelings which came over me did not lesson my concern. Generally it was just an uneasy feeling but sometimes I would become tense as a dark cloud passed through my head. For short spells I would feel unhappy for no reason. Occasionally my stomach would feel as if it was turning inside out. Such feelings were uncomfortable and bewildering.

Slowly but surely it worsened. Did this mean Mark's health was deteriorating? I had no way of knowing.

I wrestling with the anxiety, tossing it back and forth in an attempt to rationalise my thoughts. All that did was make it worse.

Reasoning that I had created this problem for myself by dwelling on it too much I tried to divert my attention in numerous ways. No matter what I tried I could not clear my mind for long. My concern had developed into a nagging worry.

Mark's reaction indicated that my hunch about his work trip was correct but I thought that regretting his plans was just the tip of the iceberg.

In the following weeks he kept popping into my head at odd moments, whenever I wasn't busy. Although I kept telling myself that he was OK and it was silly for me to think otherwise, it didn't help. Poor sleep probably played its part too.

Still the sense that I should do something persisted. And still I was bewildered by how my intuition was working. I thought it might be some form of telepathy and wondered if it could work both ways. Somehow Mark was transmitting his feelings to me so maybe I could send some to him. It was worth a try.

I decided that adopting a positive attitude would be helpful. Perhaps it could help us both? I began trying to transmit positivity to Mark whenever he popped into my head. I would deliberately focus my mind and project "Stay positive!"

I knew I would have no way of knowing if this was of any benefit to him but it certainly wasn't going to do any harm. I thought it weird, but as I was the only one who knew about it what did it matter?

After a week or so the only difference I could discern was that he came to mind even more often. I became increasingly apprehensive about Mark. Now, as well as trying to project a positive attitude, mentally, I began offering him advice. It still seemed strange and I often felt that I didn't really know what I was doing, but at least in a way I was doing something. I was doing a great deal of talking inside my own head.

"Mark, you need to be more patient; things take time."

"Sometimes you will have to compromise. You can't expect to get all you want, all the time, in your own way.

"Often processes are not straightforward, Mark. Try viewing them another way. Changing your perspective might be useful."

"You seem to be having a lot of problems but try not to dwell on them. Focus on what has been successful and continue from there."

Somehow I'd get ideas of what to say.

Naturally I was curious about my unusual intuition. I wanted some information which would both explain it and help me know what to do. My search began on internet sites. The first thing I typed into the search engine was "transfer of feeling," which led me nowhere. Then I tried "extra sensory perception" but still I found nothing. I thought telepathy might be appropriate but that proved fruitless too.

Whenever I was having a sleepless night I'd be downstairs, searching. Over a period of time I tried every word or phrase that I could come up with, including intuition, compassion, sympathy, and many things beginning with mental!

I could find information about intuition but mine was much deeper than any described. My experiences had been repetitive, lasting months and developing. I couldn't find any reference to similar occurrences.

Whichever site I transferred to, throughout these searches, there was nothing appropriate. It was very frustrating.

Three months had passed since my first intuition, without any sign of improvement.

I was still keeping busy, but every time I took a break Mark would be in my mind accompanied by the same uncomfortable feeling that he needed help and I should do something.

I longed to find something to help me or someone who understood what I was going through. We are all unique as individuals but isn't that just different combinations of common traits? And even if this trait isn't common surely it's not unknown? I couldn't be the only person to have experienced this.

I didn't want to be the only one.

I felt very alone.

The next time we were in a small group of smokers Mark seemed his usual self and I didn't sense anything amiss.

It made no sense for me still to be troubled, but the frequent awareness continued.

Towards the end of February I went to Rome with Jim. We had both looked forward to this break for some time. I also hoped it would sever this strange and unwanted connection to Mark. I was fed up with the endless yoyo effect of thinking about him and trying to stop doing so.

"It'll be different when we were there," I reasoned. "You've got yourself into the habit of thinking about him. You need to break that habit. Once we're in Rome, so far away and with plenty to do, it'll change things."

And indeed it did, but not in a way that I could possibly have predicted.

Throughout the flight my mind was distracted. I was trying to behave normally and was fine whilst Jim and I were in conversation but at other times it was extremely difficult. I was so distracted. I tried various puzzles but couldn't complete any, although they didn't seem difficult. I just couldn't think straight. When I tried reading my eyes skimmed the words without registering the text.

Eventually I gave up trying. I just let Mark into my head, because it was the easier option and I was fed up struggling against it unsuccessfully.

It was a little easier once we arrived in Rome as being busy did help, just as it had at home. But distance made no difference. I just tried to ignore the intrusions and concentrate on enjoying this holiday with Jim.

I was trying hard to dismiss Mark from my mind altogether but again this seemed to produce the opposite outcome. Now I had an almost constant awareness of him even though I wasn't sensing any particular feelings. I wasn't thinking of him all the time but somehow he was always with me, always there at the back of my mind. It was as if I was carrying him around all day long. Sometimes he would be still and quiet but he never left. It's difficult to explain it. The only thing I can compare it to is when you have a big problem. You may not think about it all the time but it's always there weighing you down. No matter what you do you cannot escape it for long until you find a solution.

By day there was so much to see and do that it was easy for me to hide how I was feeling. Each day I pretended I was my usual self though I felt far from normal. In fact I felt a little crazy. At night I would lie awake for hours, with Jim sleeping soundly beside me. Problems concerning sleeping I could handle as I don't have a regular sleep pattern and I've managed this for years. So lack of proper sleep was not what was exhausting me. It was the other problem that was taking its toll.

The whole situation was frustrating and very tiring. It had bothered me for long enough and now it was spoiling my holiday with Jim.

Over the course of a couple of days Mark seemed to gently slip from the back of my mind until he was perched on my shoulder; a burden that became increasingly heavy. As well as invading my mind it felt as if he now hunched my shoulders and bowed my head. Previously he had encroached on any times of relaxation. Now he seemed to be preventing me from relaxing in the first place.

I was tense and resentful. I just wanted Mark to leave me alone. Yet the worry continued. At the start I had felt depression was something in his future. I had not experienced any specific feelings to change this. But now I felt it was happening now. It was as if his constant presence made me conscious of it.

I worried more. I battled more. I was more frustrated. I was more tired. Pretence of normality was more difficult. More than anything else, I wanted it to end.

Nights were always the worst. One sleepless night I was feeling immensely sorry for myself. Instead of talking to Mark, mentally, I now began shouting at him, telling him to leave me alone. I was swearing, yelling, fretting, cursing. All my frustrations poured out in anger. I couldn't stand it any longer. It was driving me mad! What had I done to deserve this? How could I escape it? What was I supposed to do?

In the midst of my anguish a picture came into my head. It was a scene from the film The Green Mile showing John Coffey in his cell, a sparkling stream pouring from his mouth as he cleared his system after healing. "What am I supposed to make of that?" I asked in exasperation. "I'm not a healer so what's this about? I can't just blow it all out into the air! How am I supposed to get rid of this? What am I supposed to do?"

Strangely this was followed by an answer, "You're tired from fighting but you're fighting the wrong thing. Don't fight the worry, fight the depression."

It was as if a light shone through my darkness and things became clear. I had been wasting my energy on the wrong fight.

I remembered the anger that I'd felt after that first gut reaction. It was an anger that could fuel the fight. My fury motivated me. Depression is a demon, a despicable bully whose tricks I know. I hate this disgusting adversary who only picks on the vulnerable.

"If it's a fight you're after I'll take you on! I know you and your devious ways. I won't give in to you again and I'll help anyone who has to fight against you. I've beaten you back before and I'll do it again. You won't win!"

I know it sounds ridiculous that my mind was now speaking to depression, as if it were a person, but that is how it was. Mentally I threw down the gauntlet. My fighting thoughts had made me feel stronger and released me at last from the strangle hold of worry. As my anger abated I became calm, which was a lovely feeling after months of ongoing anxiety. Again I felt that whatever was happening to me was not harmful. It was my own approach which had caused problems.

My conviction was strong. I was resolute and calm and at last I was able to sleep, peacefully and soundly.

Next day I felt much stronger. When Mark popped into my head I simply wished him, "Good morning" very cheerfully and during the day I'd silently ask if he was enjoying the activity since he'd decided to join us on holiday! I determined once again to maintain a positive approach.

Back home my shoulders were free of their burden. Mark had gone ahead with his plans and I wasn't likely to see him for some time, so had no idea how he was feeling in reality, but I was still sensing that things were not as they should be. It still seemed that Mark never left me and the uneasy sense of him was intruding more times each day.

As the weeks passed this wore me down again. It became difficult to remain positive and self-doubt began gnawing at my resolve. It was ridiculous to be talking to someone in my head. It wasn't normal. I wasn't normal. I needed help. When I was by myself I'd continue my internet search for answers. Still I was unsuccessful.

I would often get exasperated with myself. "He's not your responsibility! Stop fretting over him, he's not a child and you are not his mother!"

Fortunately better sleep improved matters. Although I wasn't getting to sleep until the early hours I didn't waken until I'd had sufficient sleep. Being retired this was not a problem. My spirit improved and I worried less. That helped in so many ways.

I continued to occupy myself as much as possible. But gradually I realised that Mark's intrusions were developing again, with increasing frequency throughout each day. They brought a great sense of unease. It reached a point where it seemed there was little respite from Mark's interruptions to my daily life.

Night times became difficult again. Each night I would try to distract my thoughts but before long my grasshopper mind would jump back to Mark. It didn't matter how many times I diverted my thoughts, they would end up back with him.

It was my old problem of an overactive mind. Whatever I try thoughts will not shut down. I don't seem to have the same sort of on/off switch as Jim who can be asleep within minutes of closing his eyes, whereas it takes my about an hour, unless I'm ill.

It has been this way for years. Some good nights, sometimes not sleeping until the early hours and other days waking early. Generally there'll be the same pattern for several nights and then it will change. There's no order to it.

Over the years I've tried all sorts of ways to improve my sleeping; relaxation exercises, listening to music, reading, remedies, different night time routines etc. But nothing makes a consistent difference. I've been prescribed different sleeping pills and some work for a night or two but then have no effect. If the pills are strong enough to induce sleep on a regular basis they leave me feeling hung over for most of the following day, so I don't use them. Despite logging my activities, stresses, food consumption and anything else which might be the cause, nothing has proved beneficial in the long term.

Jim has grown used to this over the years. He sleeps soundly so it doesn't disturb him when I'm up in the night or when my day begins before dawn.

The problem now was that I had two of the patterns together; not being able to get to sleep for hours and also waking too early. So I'd only sleep for a couple of hours. Sometimes I slept in the day but that would make it even more difficult to sleep at night. Consequently I was thoroughly overtired, which always lowers the spirit and makes it difficult to stay positive.

I could feel myself sliding further downhill. I needed help.

Jim has always been very supportive and I knew I must talk to him, difficult though it was. I needed to tell him everything right from that evening the previous autumn.

I can't imagine what his feelings and thoughts must have been as he listened to me pouring out my extraordinary tale.

When I'd finished giving Jim the main gist of what had been happening to me he was initially sceptical, thinking maybe I was suffering some sort of obsession or infatuation. It can't have been easy for him to hear and naturally it was rather upsetting for me to talk about. As I told him more he saw how it was making me feel and agreed that it was something very unusual.

Just getting it off my chest helped a lot and I felt a great sense of relief. It was as if I had been harbouring a guilty secret for which I had no reason to feel guilty.

Still feeling very strongly that I was supposed to do something I discussed this with Jim but we couldn't come up with anything. When I told Jim how I'd been using the internet to look for answers he suggested more ideas so I undertook more computer research but still found nothing helpful.

A couple of days later I came up with an idea of something I could do. I knew Jim wouldn't be keen on it, since he'd already expressed concern at the notion of me doing anything regarding Mark. But the feeling of needing some sort of action had not diminished so I told Jim of my idea.

I realised that since I knew where Mark worked I would be able to find an address and write to him, communicating my concern.

As expected, Jim wasn't too sure about this but he could tell I needed to do something. He knows when there's a problem with anything or anyone I can't stop myself from trying to help. Although people have often said I'm a mug to put myself out, I don't see it that way. I'm not put out. Many times I've been told I'm my own worst enemy and I'm doing too much but I like being busy and get pleasure from helping. It's probably why I enjoyed teaching. It's just the way I am and Jim accepts that.

My Way

Ignoring my senses and closing my mind,
Ears that are deaf and eyes that are blind,
Turning my head and walking away,
Refusing to help? That's not my way.

"You'll be interfering! It'll do you no good."
"Mind your own business!" Well, maybe I should.
"You could get hurt. The problem's not yours."
I've heard all the warnings but I'll rise to the cause.

It may not be easy but I just have to try.
I'll consider my safety but it's hard to walk by.
It's not in my nature and I truly believe
My help is repaid by what I receive.

The simple rewards that money can't buy:
You can't purchase the smile that replaces a cry,
The tone of a voice when thanks are sincere,
Or eyes bright with light as meaning grows clear.

I think Jim also realised that this need to do something went far beyond wanting to help someone. But he was worried that there might be repercussions which could hurt me. We discussed all the possible outcomes we could think of and how they could be handled. Since I desperately needed some course of action and we could come up with no other idea, Jim eventually accepted that I had nothing to lose and should try.

So I wrote, finding it far easier than I had anticipated.

Jim read the letter and posted it for me.

CHAPTER 2
WINTER 2007/8

Unexpected Help

It was such a relief to have done something. I felt much better. I found I could relax again and I slept better. I also found that I didn't have an awareness of Mark every day, although I did still sense him occasionally.

Obviously I still thought about him and was still curious about what had happened. Although I really would have appreciated a reply, after a couple of weeks I knew I wouldn't receive one. But I still needed some sort of corroboration and rationale. The internet had yielded nothing but

I'm not very technically minded. Perhaps I hadn't been searching in the right way. It didn't mean there wasn't information available. The library was my next means of research. Over the next couple of weeks I withdraw more than a dozen books, having looked at plenty more during my visits. Once again I could find nothing that came close to my experience.

So I just had to get on with it.

The intuitive feelings kept coming and I still felt it was crazy. I was still not getting to sleep until the early hours but I didn't waken until I'd had sufficient sleep. Being retired this was not a problem. As before it gave me a lift and I felt more positive.

Crazy? So what? Many people are a bit eccentric. My intuitions were not worrying me now, in fact sometimes I found them rather amusing!

There was a period of a week or two when I'd have a sense of Mark when I walked upstairs. As this didn't happen every time I didn't anticipate it. It was always at the same point, about two thirds of the way up. After the first few times I found myself thinking of a version of the old nonsense rhyme by Hughes Mearns;

Yesterday upon the stair
I met a man who wasn't there!

He wasn't there again today.
Oh how I wish he'd go away!

It made me smile because it was so apt.

I wondered if Mark was somewhere where the lift had broken and he felt frustrated at the time and effort spent on climbing the stairs. Or maybe it was more than frustration. Maybe he found it difficult due to health problems. I didn't worry about it since the feeling I got each time was not distressing. There was no sense of anything amiss, no cause for concern, just something I found funny as it continued. It was odd.... but so was it all!

After a while I stopped sensing Mark on the stairs. Maybe that lift had been fixed? I wished something or someone would fix me!

Mark may have stopped visiting me on the stairs but I did sense him in other places, daily. I didn't tell Jim. It couldn't have been easy for him to hear that I was frequently thinking about another man. He had been very patience but I didn't want to try that patience too much. Already he'd shown more tolerance than I'd expected and I was certain that he just wanted it all over and done with. I thought he'd probably just say I should forget it now. Easier said than done!

I knew I needed to talk about my experiences without getting upset or sounding melodramatic. One day, as we were car sharing, I briefly told a friend about my strange link to Mark. She wasn't sceptical but it wasn't really an appropriate time or place to share the depth of my concern. But still it was a start.

I realized that I needed to disclose and discuss my problems fully with somebody close who was in no way involved. I knew who would help me; a very close friend who I knew would be honest and straightforward. Tina always has a sympathetic ear and I knew she would neither pander to me nor be judgemental. I could depend on her for a balanced overall view and a sensible reaction. We'd been each other's confidantes for many years and I knew that talking to her would help.

Tina listened with interest and was not at all sceptical. She didn't share my doubts and although I expressed my worries she somehow blew them away. I felt completely at ease chatting to her. She brought back my strength and determination. Relaxing in her company I felt so much better. I regained my resolve of positivity and realised that all my research was just causing frustration and negativity.

Yes, I'd continue to be curious, a curiosity which Tina shared, but I shouldn't allow this strange period of my life to overshadow the rest. I didn't need to worry any more. I'd done what I could so now I should get on with enjoying my life.

I had plenty to keep me busy. As well as my usual hobbies and chores I still had the seating to upholster for the camper. I'd also been preparing for another project which had been mooted the previous year. It was a garden makeover for a couple of friends.

I had already made a low maintenance garden for my next door neighbour. He had been through a stressful time and as he knows little about gardening it had been way down on his list of priorities. There were things which needed attention in the house too and he'd asked Jim to do some jobs for him. We were round one day discussing these when he asked me about his back garden. He had no idea where to start on the overgrown mess. We came to an arrangement. I could do the garden for him bit by bit, whenever I had time and the weather allowed. It took a couple of months, but eventually I'd completed it.

The next time we saw our friends Barbara and Ian we brought each other up to date about what we'd all been doing. Hearing of my gardening for somebody else it wasn't long before they asked if I'd do the same for them. Barbara and Ian have a much bigger plot, so it would be a longer job. But we all knew I'd love doing it.

Now their children had grown up they wanted a garden they could enjoy, with a minimum of work but plenty of colour. The space gave me plenty of scope but I'd never gardened on clay so needed to do some research. I'd looked at what was required and had already been researching which plants would be suitable for their clay soil and the different aspects. After discussing their preferences and planning the design, I was ready to start when the weather was good enough.

I could work at my own pace doing as many or as few hours as the weather and my strength would allow. The make-over was a big project and my gardening somewhat haphazard. I would have to pace myself, to avoid aggravating a back problem. Ian would do the heaviest work, moving large bags of compost and removing the loads of garden waste. The rest I could manage and enjoy, providing I was careful. I'd learned to pay attention to my back and change position regularly. I could dig, move shrubs, weed, plant, prune and water but not for long periods. Each occupation could only continue for a short while. Consequently there would be many jobs left unfinished as I took a break or changed position. It was a project that would last for months.

Gardening didn't stop me sensing Mark at various times but I didn't have any strong feelings, just uneasiness and it didn't spoil my enjoyment.

I was in my element. I was back doing something I love, the exercise was beneficial and I was out in the fresh air. Each night I'd have a good soak in a hot, fragrant bath before going to bed.

No trouble sleeping now.

Bliss!

Weeks had passed before I realised that I was sensing Mark more frequently. It must have built up slowly, unnoticed because I was busy. And possibly also because I wasn't aware of anything distressing. But they were reminders that this strange time was not yet over. Realisation brought back the frustration of not being able to find information or help.

I was totally unprepared for the help which came my way very unexpectedly.

Our singing group rehearses in a church some miles from where I live. Passing through the reception area one evening I noticed a small library of church material. There was a familiar face on one of the book covers. I recognised a friend from years before; Ken, a vicar who had lived in the next road. I'm not a church goer but had met Ken when he visited the local primary school which my children attended.

I came to know Ken well during a time of personal stress when my first marriage broke up.

My husband worked away during the week. He was living on an engineering site, having taken our small caravan up there for that purpose. There was no address and since this was before the advent of mobile phones I had no means of contacting him.

Joanne was eight, Peter five and Karen just a baby, not yet six months old. We had a large house which needed repairs and we'd just raised a loan, only six weeks previous. It was a difficult time for us all.

One evening a couple of weeks after my husband left I was surprised to see Ken at the door. One of his parishioners had told him of my situation, so he'd come to offer help. It was the first of many calls he made over the next few years. Ken was a quiet man, a good listener and he offered me good counsel.

When he was about to leave that first night Ken asked, "May I say a prayer for you all? I know you don't believe but..."

I interrupted him. "It's not that I don't believe, Ken. I have quite strong beliefs. It's just that they don't fit into any specific religion. I know a little bit about a number of religions from having to teach about them. I've found parts that I agree with in all of them but none exactly suit me so I don't follow any one in particular. I have my own ideas about God."

"Yes," he replied, "I think most people have their own idea of God."

I closed my eyes, listened as he prayed and thanked him for his thoughts and his kindness.

It was the first of many visits. He didn't come on a regular basis but would pop round at different times every week or two. With each visit I felt I understood more of the meaning of Christianity. I learnt more from Ken than I had from the years of Sunday school, scripture lessons, Bible and communion classes, and the church attendance of my youth. Yet we never discussed religion. Ken's teaching came from his demeanour, his consideration, his advice and encouragement. It came not from preaching but by example and conversation. He brought a sense of peace and comfort and was a kind friend to me and the children.

Even when he'd retired and moved away he would still visit occasionally. I was frequently surprised by his timing. It was as if he knew whenever I was really troubled. Sometimes it would about be a problem I had not discussed with anyone, so no one could have told him. Yet somehow my need was communicated to him. I had frequently remarked upon his uncanny awareness. Ken would just smile.

Clearly there *are* ways of knowing things that cannot be fully explained.

Eventually we'd lost touch, so I hadn't known of Ken's death. The book I spotted was written by his widow, with the support of the church, in memory of Ken. Reading the short account of his life, I learnt of the health problems and other difficulties which Ken had overcome during his life in Britain and abroad. And something of the work he had accomplished in many ministries.

I had been privileged to know Ken, to have received his advice, help and support. I said a much belated prayer in memory of the quiet, unassuming man, for whom I had the greatest respect.

As I'd told Ken, I have my own ideas about God. I don't believe in any one true faith to the exclusion of all others. But I do consider faith and belief to be powerful and important. Although I am not religious, I think that following a common interest or belief is beneficial in bringing people together and creating support groups.

But to me god is neither male nor female, not from any particular race or class or of any age. I think that god is in all of us, in our soul or spirit or conscience. I'm not sure where it dwells.

I've found a simplistic way to describe what I believe. It's not based on any scriptures or texts but from a much more humble source; an advert and my liking for playing around with words!

The advertised product was described as being good with nought taken out, so ...... take the word "good," remove "o" and what do you get?

I believe that people are born "good" but life experiences influence us all. The god in whom I believe is pure goodness; a perfection which is impossible to achieve yet a concept which can be followed.

I can't recall how long it is that I have felt this way, but I think Ken's visits played a large part in making me think about what I really believe. Thinking of

Ken gave me strength. His guidance always made me feel more positive. In his calm and gentle way he always portrayed a sense of trust that things would eventually settle into a better balance.

Although I still didn't understand what was happening to me, the sense that it was not harmful and had some good purpose was reinforced. In the past Ken had inexplicably known when I'd needed extra help, so what I was now experiencing could have a similar source.

Ken had inspired in me the determination to cope. Now I felt he was helping me once more; directing my thoughts to considering what I believed about the current situation. Then to consider the problem again and the strategies which helped.

I believed there was some purpose to what was happening to me,

I believed that it was not harmful but good.

I believed that Mark was suffering from depression.

I believe that sometimes we instinctively know things which we have no explicable way of knowing.

I believe that science cannot explain everything and some things are beyond the grasp of our reasoning.

When I had believed in my feelings I had felt strong not burdened.

When I had followed my instincts I was not troubled.

My problems stemmed from self-doubt.

My own lack of confidence brought the fears and worries. So I needed to stop doubting, follow my instincts and accept this burden.

I had to change my thinking until I no longer had a burden, but a purpose.

I needed to free my mind of doubt and believe in what I was doing, have faith and the courage of my convictions.

I should use the strength of purpose positively by ensuring that nothing harmful could occur through my actions.

Once again, Ken had guided me and given me strength so once again, from my heart, I thanked him for all his help.

My Beliefs

I follow no religion
Though my beliefs are strong.
I put my faith in goodness
But sometimes we all go wrong.

I believe in helping others
For societies to thrive.
We all need other people
To share interests and drive.

I believe in promoting happiness.
Sadness and stress is destructive.
With contentment and enjoyment
We can be much more productive.

I believe in the freedom of speech
For opinion to be expressed,
But I don't believe we have the right
To prey on the weak or distressed.

I believe that power can corrupt
And spawn man's selfish greed.
Mankind rapes our planet
Yet the poor still live in need.

I believe in the power of love
As a deep and driving force
But what love will accomplish
Depends upon its source.

Dot Streets

By now it was April and intermittent wet weather prevented gardening every day but I still had plenty to keep me busy. As well as attending art classes I sketched and painted at home, there were songs to be learned for the next concert, and having completed the sewing for the camper I had agreed to help with another sewing project which would take some weeks to complete. And of course there were always jobs around the house.

With my time fully occupied it was when I took a break that I would often have an awareness of Mark. Sometimes I could sense he was alright but other times I'd have an uneasy feeling. Since the intrusions were not persistent I found I could cope quite easily at first but as the weeks passed self-doubt crept in again. I really needed to know if I'd done the right thing. What if writing to him had been wrong? What if I was misinterpreted all this?

I tried to banish such doubts but lack of proper sleep was pulling me down. Jim knew I was very tired. I kept assuring him that I wasn't overdoing things. Whenever I returned home from my gardening exploits Jim would want me to have a rest. I didn't argue with him.

Sitting by the window looking out one bright afternoon I was contemplating what I needed to do next in Barbara and Ian's garden and what still needed attention in my own. I was appreciating the changes which each new spring day brought and enjoying watching the birds feeding.

Tired but nicely relaxed I was gently beginning to doze when I heard a voice in my head. It was not like a thought entering my consciousness but as if Mark was speaking to me, telling me quietly but most emphatically, "I don't want to come back! I want to stay here." It was clearly his voice and he sounded very down hearted.

I was wide awake immediately. This was something new. I'd been talking to Mark in my head on and off for months but never had, nor expected, a response that I could hear.

I knew Mark was still away on his business trip and what I heard seemed very strange. This was the trip that I thought he didn't want to go on! If he hadn't really wanted to go then surely he'd be pleased to be returning. Maybe I really had got it all wrong. It was both intriguing and frustrating.

I was pleased that Mark would soon be back. Although I had no idea when I would see him, I knew I would eventually. At some point I would have the opportunity to discover if I'd made the right decision in writing to him. Obviously it would be embarrassing if he had been baffled by my letter. Whatever the outcome I needed to know.

The following week another unusual thing happened. At a rehearsal I was told me where Mark would be at a particular time and date. And I had a reason to be in the same location apart from wanting to speak to him.

I had to take advantage of this opportunity. I didn't discuss it with Jim. Since first talking to him about my problem I'd kept my mental anguish to myself. Jim knew that I'd felt better after I'd written to Mark so I'd left it at that. My decision to go was made easier by knowing that Jim would be out at the time. I was sure to be back before him. I would be able to tell him when he came home and maybe we could put this episode behind us.

I set out with my feelings in turmoil. After all these months I would have an answer. I was excited but also very nervous. I just tried to concentrate on my driving, my hands tightly gripping the steering wheel because I felt shaky.

As I parked near my destination I couldn't believe who was just getting out of the car two from mine! I took a couple of minutes to compose myself as much as I could before leaving the car.

Summoning up all my courage I approached Mark and after explaining my reason for being there I identified myself as the person who'd written, asking, "You got my letter?"

Suddenly we were both speaking at once, neither of us looking at the other. I was babbling in my nervousness. Mark, head down, was crushing his cigarette underfoot. I didn't take in what he was saying but as he straightened up he apologised for not recognising me. Then reaching his hand towards me and staring straight into my eyes, he said, with clear sincerity, "Thank you *so* much."

It was such a relief to know that I'd been right to be concerned. That gave me the courage to ask about what I'd heard him saying, in my head, just the previous week; that he hadn't wanted to return.

"How did you know?" he responded, stepping back a few paces and turning away. Then he looked back at me asking, "Who's been talking?" This time he sounded annoyed.

"No one has said anything! *You* told me!" I replied, "Like I said, it was your voice in my head. I know it seems weird and I have wondered if I'm crazy!"

At that he approached me again, no longer annoyed but looking astonished.

"You are not crazy" he told me. "It's true."

He told me of other things which had happened during his trip, asking if I knew about them. I generally didn't, though they didn't surprise me as they fitted in with the feelings I'd been picking up and I told him so.

Once again I voiced the doubts I'd been harbouring.

"I've felt like I'm going mad!"

Once again Mark assured me that I wasn't. So I went on, "There are other things that I've just sensed."

As I described them he kept turning away, clearly surprised or even shocked. He'd step back sometimes holding his head in his hands. Often he'd shake his head too, though not to deny what I was saying for each time he turned back to me to confirm that each thing had been true. It was an interesting, unusual and difficult conversation, not because there was any awkwardness between us but because we weren't anywhere private. We were on a pathway and often had to halt our conversation, moving to let people pass by.

The rehearsal was due to begin, so time was short. I kept reminding him but he obviously wasn't concerned with time keeping. As we continued talking Mark told me some positive things about his trip, which he hadn't anticipated and had rid him of his previous apprehensions. He looked and sounded fine.

Mark had recovered from the initial shock and I was satisfied that I had been right in what I'd sensed. In other circumstances we would have continued talking but I had taken up enough of his time. I knew that he was already late for his rehearsal, so I said goodbye, gave him a hug and told him to take care.

Returning to the car I sat having a cigarette, attempting to calm myself before driving away. But Mark was in no hurry to leave. Coming to my car he began explaining the reasons for some of the emotion I'd sensed. Even when I said goodbye again and set off he stood watching, looking very thoughtful.

I think we'd both have appreciated more time to talk but I couldn't hold him up any further. I wondered if there'd ever be a chance to resume the conversation. I didn't think so. It had been such an odd mix of revelations, interruptions and confirmations between two people who didn't really know each other. Too unusual and unique, I felt, to be continued in the future.

But I had the confirmation I hoped for.

The relief was overwhelming. A great burden had been lifted and I was over the moon. When Jim arrived home, I contained myself at first, asking about his evening. But before long my excitement took over. I couldn't hold it in any longer.

I brought Jim up to date, probably not very coherently, between giggles and comments like; "I was right!" and "I'm not crazy!" I really can't say how Jim responded to any particular part but I know he said how pleased he was for me.

There were no recriminations that I hadn't talked to him about it, and I didn't regret having spared Jim the worry and helplessness that I know he would have felt. We just hugged. Although we didn't express it in words I know we both thought this was closure and I'd now get back to being myself again.

How wrong we were!

CHAPTER 3
SPRING 2008

The Picture

Next morning I woke with the bliss of having slept really well. Relaxed and happy, content and well, I lay in bed whilst Jim showered. My thoughts varied between remembering the previous evening and contemplating how to spend this lovely day.

First I would just enjoy these moments. Turning onto my side I snuggled myself back into the bedclothes. I could easily have dozed off again but didn't want to. I'd had enough of playing catch up on sleep. I didn't want to waste any of the day ahead. I stretched out and opened my eyes.

Shock hit me as I took in another unexpected and unprecedented revelation.

On the wardrobe door was a picture. It resembled a print of an old black and white photograph, raggedly torn in half from top to bottom. Only the left hand side was displayed.

There were many people looking out from the scene but they were somewhat unreal in frozen stillness, with their mouths open. They gave the picture an eerie atmosphere. But it was Mark who drew my attention. He didn't seem frozen like the others, in fact it was almost as if he was twitching. He was sitting awkwardly with his back to most people. He seemed to be trying to distance himself from those in front of him. His shoulders were hunched, his head tilted down as if he didn't want to look at anything. He held one hand to his face, which looked gaunt. With his knees drawn up towards his body he appeared cowed and exhausted, trying to hide.

What had the worst effect on me was the sickening feeling of fear which accompanied the scene.

I closed my eyes and when I looked again there was just the wardrobe door, as usual.

I had to compose myself. I knew I wasn't going to tell Jim about this. I was determined not to be brought down again though I couldn't deny the fear which I'd felt. I had to fight that and think rationally.

I didn't recognise the scene but I had the impression that it was a future event; a rehearsal or performance. The picture haunted me and came to mind often but I was determined not to be scared. Whenever I visualised it I deliberately made myself review it and fight the fear. Each time was easier than before though it took three days before I could recall the scene unemotionally.

During that time other things escalated quickly.

The morning after this vision, Mark was back in my mind even as I woke. During the day I found I was picking up his emotions more frequently, and with greater force. No matter what I tried doing to keep myself occupied, I couldn't block him out for long. The slightest break in my activities and I'd sense him again. I didn't just know intuitively how he felt, I experienced the feelings myself; worry, discomfort, apprehension, frustration. None of the emotions were good. And I was sure that these feelings weren't part of Mark's future but how he felt now. My concern for him grew but I didn't sense that I was meant to do anything this time.

I had felt so good after Mark had confirmed my feelings. I had felt so relieved and so happy but there had been so little time to appreciate feeling good.

The following day began the same with Mark back in my mind before I had even opened my eyes properly. I woke every morning with him instantly in my head and the sense of him would always be accompanied by a feeling of great anxiety. Always negative feelings which were so strong that they would overwhelm me. Although they didn't last long they were occurring a number of times daily.

Each day there would be longer times when my own feelings would be subjugated by his.

Recalling my strange experience in Rome I knew I had to pick my battle wisely. Stay positive. Don't let it get you down. Fight the depression but remember it isn't yours. Remember that your instincts have been right.

Now I fought a different battle: not to let this overcome me.

I had to hang on to my beliefs more than ever.

I struggled on, each day becoming more nervous, fretful, anxious and fearful.

My greatest worry now was that Mark was heading for a really bad time, worse than before. Since his emotions were now overwhelming my own, I was apprehensive about what the future held for me, too.

Again night-time was the worst. I knew I had to stay positive. It was important not to be scared. I had made myself fight my fear over that picture on my wardrobe. I could still visualise it in my head without feeling frightened. Although it had taken three days, I had managed to fight the fear. So I had that success to underpin my current fight.

Somehow I had to ride this storm and not be overwhelmed. It wasn't easy when I was increasing battered by Mark's feelings. As they came and went I was in a constant state of change, one minute myself and the next hit by Mark's emotions.

I was reeling from the shocks and needed time to build up my strength.

When I'd seen the picture and fought the fear successfully it had been after a huge sense of relief, self-belief and positivity, followed by a really good night's sleep. Now I was weary before I began and the bombardment had continued with increasing force, still beginning as soon as I awoke. These feelings were not always bad but were seldom good. It was clear that Mark was very unsettled, to say the least. With his feelings completely crushing my own, I was very unsettled too. It was extremely tiring, particularly as I was trying to maintain a front of normality.

I was exhausted.

I worried about what to do. I worried about what I could do. I worried about Mark's health and I worried about my own. In six days, since seeing Mark, I had gone from extreme high to desperately low.

It was obvious that I couldn't go on this way. The thought of depression was ever present. I'd vowed to beat it but no longer felt strong enough for the fight. It wasn't my depression but it was having an increasing effect on me. If Mark did succumb and his feelings overwhelmed me I would suffer that invidious invader once more.

I felt I needed to see Mark again.

This time I decided to talk to Jim about it first. I had to stop trying to appear normal. Dropping the pretence had helped before so I hoped it would again. But I knew it would be more difficult this time. Intuition is one thing, but hearing a voice in my head was so much more. And seeing that picture was surely psychic.

There lay the difficulty. I knew that Jim had always been wary, maybe scared, of anything psychic, feeling no good would come of it. I knew he'd want to back away and not hear.

It couldn't be helped. I had to tell him. I needed to stop pretending and open up.

I didn't pick my moment or try any sensible approach. I think I was beyond being sensible. I just began blurting it all out to Jim. As expected he was reluctant to hear me, but I carried on talking, following him around. The more I talked the more upset I became and the more annoyed Jim became. Before long he'd had enough.

"Stop this!" he demanded, "Stop getting yourself into such a state!"

I didn't seem able to stop. Flood gates had opened. All my worries, doubts, and fears gushed out, making me even more distressed and Jim even more cross.

"What's the point of all this? Stop thinking about him. Do you think he's worried about you? I bet he never even gives you a second thought!" Jim was almost shouting now.

"I don't know what the point is!" I answered through my tears. "I've never known and you know that. I don't understand it but I can't stop it."

The more I tried to explain the more frantic I became. "I can't control it. I don't know what's happening to me."

"Control yourself then, because carrying on like this you're only going to make yourself ill and I'll be the one you expect to look after you. Well think again! There's no need for all this."

"Do you think I want to be ill? Do you think I want to go through that again?

I was distraught at the idea of depression again. So much for my fighting talk about not letting it beat me. I was in a state just thinking about it!

The more he heard the more Jim seemed to back way, clearly shocked by my state, scared himself and feeling helpless in a situation which was out of control. As soon as I mentioned seeing Mark again Jim was against it. He was adamant that I shouldn't go. He didn't want the situation to escalate any further. Jim insisted that what I needed was to calm down, look to my own needs and definitely not see Mark. He kept repeating that I was working myself into just the sort of state that could lead me into depression.

Finally he could take no more. "It's up to you because you can do what you want and I won't stop you!" He flung the words at me as he strode away. I didn't follow him. I realised that I'd said all I could.

We don't often argue, but when we do we need our own space for a while afterwards, to calm down and think rationally. I needed to do that now.

Jim was right. What he'd said was true. Neither of us attempted to control the other. We were each free to do as we wanted. I needed to be sure that what I chose to do was the right thing.

Gradually I began to be able to process things more clearly. I did need to get a grip and stop worrying about something that might not happen. I was exhausted and scared so maybe I wasn't seeing or sensing things properly. What could I tell Mark anyway? I hadn't been able to identify the setting of the picture and only thought it was sometime in the future. What would be the point of telling him that?

Jim would be upset if I went and it would be unfair of me. I'd felt from the start that this wasn't my depression, so it would only become mine if I allowed that to happen. I'd also sensed from the start that whatever this was all about it was not harmful. So if any harm was to come to me it would be through my own actions, not from my intuition.

That's what it amounted to really. And it would be unfair for Jim to have to cope if I let myself get depressed.

Although my most serious bouts of depression had occurred before I met Jim, he'd had to contend with the aftermath. When we met I had only been back at work for a few weeks after an absence of seven months. The immediate stresses had been dealt with but there were other underlying problems. I'd been hurt by relationships in the past and lacked the confidence to commit again. I know I was often unreasonable and don't know how Jim put up with it, but he was so good to and for me. And for the children, who had naturally been affected too. It was a difficult time for us all and it was Jim's fortitude, tolerance and good humour that saw us through.

About eighteen months into our marriage I realised that I still had too many unresolved issues from my past. I'd thought I'd buried them but I'd come to appreciate that doing that was not a solution. My past was still affecting me. It was the reason I seemed, unintentionally, to keep testing Jim when I didn't have to. Afterwards I'd feel guilty. That would make me feel bad, which would make me feel unworthy so I couldn't believe that Jim could possibly love me. The circle would be complete and off I'd go again; the testing followed by the guilt, the unworthiness, the neediness and back to testing. Jim hadn't deserved any of that and I had wanted to break this circle, which was unhealthy and unfair.

It was up to me to stop the horrible cycle, so I had made an appointment with the doctor, who increased my medication and referred me for therapy. A course of counselling followed. The weekly sessions were not easy and always churned up a variety of emotions. Jim had been a much needed support during the long course.

A few years later I'd had more counselling sessions to counter stress, which again was not Jim's fault. His kindness and consideration helped my through, though I couldn't have made life easy for him. His love and support had been vital to me as I fought to overcome my problems.

He deserved better than to be almost threatened with fears regarding someone else.

Another consideration was Jim's own health. He'd had a heart attack a few years previously, followed by quadruple heart by-pass surgery. Although he's made a good recovery he has to take numerous tablets and cope with the side effects. He no longer has the confidence or tolerance he'd had during the earlier years of our marriage.

Our roles had changed with Jim now needing my help and support to stay positive. I hadn't been giving any of that or anything else. What had I been doing to him? Rather than giving him any of the support he needed, recently I'd withdrawn myself. I thought I'd been protecting him but how was he to know that? I hadn't thought clearly. My mind had been too focussed elsewhere.

I came down to earth with a terrific bump!

So in the end my decision was a no-brainer really. Just as well too since my brain had clearly not been working well!

I needed to get my priorities back in place and keep them there.

When I told Jim I wouldn't be going to see Mark he was bothered that I had made this decision reluctantly, would get in a state about that and blame him. I soon put him straight!

Taking stock made me see how quickly I'd been brought down. From the euphoria of knowing I wasn't crazy I had descended rapidly to become a frightened creature, sobbing, shouting, and expecting to succumb to mental illness. All in within a week!

Ridiculous!

I was riding an emotional roller coaster and I had to level it out as much as possible. The way I'd been reacting had resulted in a fast drop from the heights and a shocking plummet towards the bottom. I needed to put the brakes on, slow things down and try to get as straight as possible, as quickly as possible. I simply had to exercise some control and try to stay positive. (Did I say "simply"? Surely I should have known better!)

My determination returned and I made some more decisions:

I would tell Jim about what I was experiencing, in a matter of fact way without getting emotional. I thought this would help us both.

I wouldn't dwell on what the future might bring and work myself into a frenzy but concentrate on the present and the people and things which gave me pleasure.

I'd try to block out thoughts of Mark so that I'd know for sure that I wasn't doing any of this to myself.

So I started a new approach.

Identification came first. Which were his emotion and which were mine? Since I'd been approaching the situation emotionally, I'd added my own feelings and caused more aggravation. I had to keep Mark's feelings separate from my own as much as possible and then try to tackle the problem quickly. This was easier if I could identified a reason for my own emotions to shift. But this was rarely the case. With no way of knowing any of the causes for Mark's feelings I could only consider what to do about whatever I sensed. Ignoring it didn't work because, like a nagging headache it would just persist and often worsen. I hadn't found a way to dismiss or block my intuitions, so I had to accept them and consider a reaction.

I decided I would spend a few minutes paying attention, follow my instincts and then continue with whatever I was doing. I'd have a deliberate approach and not let the distractions take up so much time.

I continued to wake with Mark in my head. I acknowledged that without fighting it and would focus on him for a few minutes. I found that this awareness was not accompanied by any intuitive feeling, it was just that Mark was there. The days continued in their up and down way, and I did sense how Mark was feeling at various times during each day. I stuck to my plan and it worked, limiting the length of time when his emotions overwhelmed me. However, it didn't limit the number of interruptions. It was almost like having an attention seeking child! Given a little attention the pestering would stop more quickly, but it would return. It was wearing and frustrating but definitely an improvement. I managed to avoid getting into a frenzy.

Getting to sleep was difficult as I couldn't shift Mark from my head. It was then that I found further intuition came into play.

Instead of talking to him, I sometimes found I was visualising something which might help. I'd imagine him walking in a wood or along a beach. Maybe a trip to explore a new place, to go fishing, or watch a film. I'd see him having a shoulder and neck massage or I'd do breathing exercises myself and picture him doing them. They weren't ideas that I thought out, just whatever popped into my head.

It all seemed rather silly but again it wasn't going to hurt anyone, so I didn't let it bother me. I just got on with it as I'd promised myself, trying yet again to remain positive and remember that these problems were not really mine.

I don't recall how long I continued doing this and of course I had no way of knowing if it helped Mark, but it certainly worked for me. As my thoughts drifted through these relaxing activities I would gradually relax and fall asleep. I had a few good nights until the pattern changed again.

The early hours can be the darkest so if I wasn't asleep by 2a.m. or thereabouts I'd get up. Sometimes I'd read or do puzzles, some nights I would be back Googling, exploring other pathways, always hoping but not succeeding.

Then a different pattern began.

I found that just as I was dozing off to sleep, no matter what the hour, something would approach my slumbering consciousness as if from a distant horizon, not troubling me but catching at my last bit of sleepy attention. It would resonate and then work into a rhythmic word or line, repeating over and over. As it grew stronger I would begin to waken again, finding a connection, maybe an idea which linked, or a rhyming word, sometimes another line.

These were always repeated and repeated in a rhythm until I was fully awake. Sleep now became impossible as I was impelled to get up and write the lines, get them out of my head, onto paper and arrange the next line.

And so began sessions of writing verse. It isn't something I usually do, although there had been a short while, some years previous, when I'd had a spell of writing poems. Very occasionally I had written others, usually for a specific purpose.

This time I didn't need to complete the verses. I would just work on them until I knew I'd be able to sleep. Many of these lines were soon discarded but some I kept and completed later.

In some way they would all be connected to Mark but were also an outlet for my own feelings, some deep and dark but others light-hearted.

The Impossible Creature

You're the impossible creature of whom I should not think,
You know the one I'm meaning; that elephant that's pink.

You're the irritating itch I cannot scratch away,
Always just beyond my reach as another nerve you play.

You're the unfinished puzzle with such perplexing clues
They baffle my intelligence, always tending to confuse.

You're the incessant jingle playing around my head.
When I think at last it's over I find you're back instead.

You're an extraordinary mystery in which I'm now involved.
A case remaining open until all the clues are solved.

Mark's presence continued, but changed. I no longer woke with him in my mind. Awareness of him wasn't a daily occurrence or regular in any way. Some days I'd sense him a few times but other days not at all. Unlike my previous intuitions there was nothing worrying, no sense of needing to do anything, nothing intense. After a few weeks I wondered why I was still feeling this connection at all, since there seemed to be no problems now.

So why wasn't it over? Why couldn't I just let go? Was it just my curiosity getting the better of me now? Was the awareness really just my own thoughts?

I realised that I needed to have another perspective on the whole subject; a viewpoint from someone not involved or affected by this strange situation.

I have one friend who has a strong intuitive sense. She might have a sense of unease on meeting someone who is hiding the truth very plausibly. Or she may think of someone and have a curious, unexpected idea about them. Then time will reveal that she was right. She has faith in her intuitive feelings even though there may be no outward indication to support what she senses. She may not divulge her intuition, but she doesn't doubt such feelings.

Jane and I had become friends during the many years we had taught together. Now I was retired, but as Jane was still teaching it was usually during the holidays that we caught up on each other's news. When we met up during the Easter break, I told her everything, aware that she'd have a better understanding than most.

She was fascinated by my story, shared some more of her own and we embraced our own, unusual experiences in friendship. We laughed and joked together, which was just what I'd needed. I felt more relaxed and positive once more.

My odd sleeping patterns continued and I was often on my laptop in the early hours, writing. I was determined to stay as upbeat as possible, so concentrated on the peculiarities of the situation rather that the worries.

Occasionally I would spend a night not on rhymes, but back on the laptop still looking for information to help. From the start I'd found that psychic sites often came up in my searches. I know that we are all psychic to some degree. I have an open mind on such matters. I have always harboured some interest, but have never delved into the subject. Psychic sites had often come up during my internet searches but I didn't want a reading or training, which was generally what was offered. After the variations of my experiences I couldn't deny a psychic link and knew I needed to explore further, though I was a little reluctant to do this.

My unwillingness stems from my childhood, despite knowing that I had had a small psychic experience as a child.

When I was about 8 years old, my uncle was admitted to hospital. I'd heard my parents say that this was most unexpected, since he'd had never had a day's illness in his life. A couple of days later I was walking across the landing, from my bedroom to the bathroom, when the phone rang. It was just after 8am, not a time we usually received calls. I knew immediately that it was news of my uncle's death.

When my parents told me, I didn't say that I already knew. I didn't think I'd be believed and would probably get in trouble.

As I grew older I learned that my uncle's widow proclaimed to be psychic. She was mum's younger sister and always wanted mum to join her at meetings or readings. My father was very much against this, so it caused rows. In the past, mum had sometimes accompanied my aunt and she used to tell me of things which had happened on these occasions. I found it all fascinating. Mum knew she had my attention and would tell me more and more. I was often astonished by her revelations of what had occurred and what she had discovered, often in the strangest of ways.

It also turned out that my cousin was more psychic than her mother, which caused a mix of both pride and jealousy. Another cause of aggravation in the family.

My cousin didn't have a very happy life. Eventually she was diagnosed as schizophrenic and became an alcoholic, though I don't know in which order. She died, too young, in a house fire.

All this had put me off investigating anything psychic, but I couldn't put this off any longer. I looked up information about clairvoyance and clairsentience, but still found no examples of people with experiences similar to my own. Whichever way I explored the many psychic sites, I found nothing of relevance. I would also check on sites I'd previously tried, to see if there were any updates. Still my endeavours were always fruitless.

I tried not to get frustrated, but it seemed so improbable that there was no record of anything similar. In fact it seemed impossible.

Although I never doubted my initial intuition, I still had many doubts about the whole situation and my handling of it, still wondering if I was responsible in some subconscious way for all the odd things I was experiencing. I knew I had often been over-thinking it all. Dwelling too much on my thoughts could have created a false impression for me. Maybe it had been my own fanciful imagination that was making too much of it all. Months previously I'd wondered if I was doing this to myself and Jim had too when I'd first talked to him. We had discussed this but we couldn't see how it might be self-inflicted. Certainly I wasn't doing it deliberately but perhaps subconsciously?

How could I know?

It wasn't long before I found out. Once again discovery came from an unexpected source: our beloved dog, Benji.

He had been chosen and bought by Jim for our youngest, Karen, who been asking for a dog for some time. Both Jim and I had always had dogs and Karen hadn't known life without a canine friend until the passing of our previous dog, Pepper, who had belonged to Peter.

A rescue dog from the local pound, Benji was a Jack Russel terrier cross who had been a stray found in a local park. Jim had picked him out at the pound because he was so appealing and clearly had character. Having put his name down as a prospective owner, Jim took us to the pound for Karen to see if she'd like this little white and black mongrel. I'm not sure if she would have picked him out herself from the wide range available since she was reduced to tears by the plight of all the dogs who would still be left behind with an uncertain future.

A few days later we collected the little ~~terror~~ terrier. As soon as we arrived home we found just how much of a madcap character he was. Our hall was large and he ran a few circles around there, picking up speed before charging through the open door to the front room, jumping over the back of the settee like a steeplechaser, clearing the seat. and landing on the coffee table. Fortunately this was empty, since he slid across it diagonally, on his stomach with his legs spayed out. He then nosedived to the floor. It was like watching a real life Disney cartoon.

The first time Jim and I took Benji out for a walk, it was obvious why he had been a stray. He'd run to any other dog he saw, playing until he spotted another to charge after. The walk ended up being mostly a run as we chased after him. Whenever we caught up he'd run towards us, circle us and then be off again. It took a long time to get him back on his lead that day. Exercising the dog would certainly make us fit. But clearly Benji would need to be kept on a lead, until he learned to respond to his new name and not run away.

Karen began taking him to dog training classes and he learned to socialise with people, be less dog orientated and respond to his name. However, his socialisation classes had been too successful. He now liked meeting people as much as he did other dogs. Any open door was an invitation for him, be it house, car or caravan. It was very embarrassing. So many times we had to retrieve Benji and apologise for him but very rarely were people bothered by his intrusion. Like us, they found him appealing and were quite happy to fuss and feed him. Wherever he went he'd make new friends, canine or human. He was a funny, independent little terrier mongrel who loved life. Very little troubled Ben.

One day, obviously hoping we were about to take him out, Ben jumped into the car quite undeterred that he'd mistaken the open bonnet for the boot! He had a good look at the engine before happily settled down and was very disappointed to be removed and returned inside.

In a country park one day Ben had jumped onto the top of a wall, walking along the broad top until he reached a section where the wall had collapsed. He jumped down on the other side and I stepped across, noticing a lady standing watching. Clearly no dog walker, she wore a wide brimmed blue hat, festooned with feather trim, and a three-quarter length, light brown fur coat.

Between us was a wide stretch of mud, which Benji had run straight into, his legs, tail and stomach now thick with the gooey black mess. "Oh no! Ben," I yelled. "Come back here."

Not looking at me but still watching Ben, the lady called, in a far back voice, "Oooooh, isn't he just adorable." Bending slightly she began to pat her knees. She was encouraging my filthy and probably smelly dog to go to her! Fortunately the depth and thickness of the mud was hampering his progress a great deal so he could only move slowly.

"Please don't let him near you!" I pleaded," Look at the state of him. He'll ruin your coat!"

"But I simply lu-u-u-v him! I want to take him home with me."

She continued patting her knees to encourage him but there was no way I would let her fur coat meet his!

Calling Benji to me, I made my way back over the gap in the sandstone wall and began to run, still shouting constantly and looking behind me. Thank goodness Ben chased after me, finding an area of clean grass where he could roll about to clean himself of much of the mud. He didn't mind getting dirty but never liked to stay that way.

Nothing phased Ben, he simply loved life, but he did give us some heart-stopping moments.

Spotting our family on the beach one day Ben jumped off the edge of the promenade! I had him on the lead at the time, so his leap was brought up short very quickly. Benji's bungie jump! I let go of his lead and watched, apprehensively as he fell the rest of the way. Landing on a mix of sand and pebbles he just stood up, shook himself and ran, tail wagging happily, to join the others.

Times when my heart was in my mouth thinking of the outcome of his actions always ended, luckily, without problems. Naughty and nosy as he was, he did make us laugh. We often said, if we'd had a recorder we could have made a fortune selling videos of his escapades.

As Ben aged he developed health problems and we were advised to cut down on the exercise and not let him jump. The first was easy, but not the second, since Ben would jump and bounce whenever he was exited. Nothing was going to stop him from chasing a group of birds, jumping as high as he could when they flew off. We could never make out whether he wanted to catch one or fly himself!

Less exercise was not to his liking so he'd quickly and quietly escape if he could and find someone to play with. This led to many searches and a lot of worry until we'd receive a phone call and discover what he'd been up to.

One time the call was from the school at the bottom of our road. Ben had found a way into the playground at playtime, enjoyed the children fussing him and then followed them inside for lessons.

Once he headed for his favourite park but was stopped by a shop keeper who opened a packet from her shelf to feed him treats!

Another time a lady from the next road called us after Ben had entered their garage, where her husband was working on the car. From there he accessed their back garden, chased their cat out, trotted into the house and helped himself to the cat's milk and food. When I arrived, very embarrassed and full of apologies, she was stroking Ben as she fed him cat treats. She was clearly amused by his antics. He'd made yet another human friend but probably a feline enemy too.

Despite all the liberties he took we only had two complaints about him in thirteen years.

As he aged, his eyesight gradually deteriorated, which led to some mishaps as he'd run into things. These misadventures also worsened as time passed.

One bright spring afternoon, we went to the beach for Jim to take photos of the lighthouse, which I wanted to paint. Ben enjoyed a run on the sand. In this area there is also a fort and a marine lake with a pathway around it. There was nobody else around until a couple of lifeboat men strolled down from the nearby station. The four of us were chatting when suddenly the weather changed from sunshine to dark clouds, wind and the start of rain. We all moved to the shelter of the fort and continued our conversation. Ben wandered around, exploring and then returned to. He proceeded to cock his leg, not on the wall, but on the leg of one of the men. Jim and I were both embarrassed and apologetic, but the lifeboat man just laughed, said he'd experienced worse and it didn't matter as he was wearing his waterproofs!

Soon afterwards the heavens opened. We parted company with the men, Jim and I turning to the pathway calling Ben, who came running. But he didn't turn onto the path, instead he continued straight ahead, right under the railings and plunging into the marine lake! We were both shouting his name as he surfaced and began swimming. I realised he would not be able to identify the slipway which was his means of exit. Dashing to it, I yelled his name as loud as I could, continuing to do so until he was swimming in the right direction and could touch ground. He ran to me and, after a good shake, he was happy to have his lead on. We headed back to the car with Ben pulling on his lead, shivered all the way in the pouring rain and strong wind. At the car we were able to dry him and wrap him up. Back home he took to his bed and slept.

Jim and I both felt sure that this would be the end, but Ben wasn't ready to give up yet. After a couple of days nursing he was back on his feet. Rather than weakening him, the shock seemed to have had the opposite effect and given Ben a new lease of life.

We had said good bye to him a few times in his last years but Benji came through operations successfully and survived to continue enjoying life, albeit at a slower pace.

Over the years Ben had clearly decided he was mine and as he aged he sometimes wouldn't leave the house unless I was going too. Often these would be times when I wasn't feeling too good and it seemed Benji could sense how I was feeling. During difficult times he'd rarely leave my side, lying at my feet or putting his head on my lap, being quiet rather than his usual madcap self. He would stay by me whenever he could and only go out if I was with him, even if it meant missing a walk.

One Saturday in June Jim and I had tickets for a ball, to celebrate the singing company's 10th anniversary. Since this was held in Leeds we had booked into a hotel for the night. Our son Peter and his wife, Becky, would stay at our house to mind Ben.

That morning I'd been to the hairdressers and Benji greeted me as heartily as ever on my return. This would usually result in him having a fit of coughing. The vet had explained that this was a means of regulating his heart, as Ben had a heart murmur. But this time there was no coughing. Ben just slowly walked into the back room. By the time I'd hung up my coat and followed, he had collapsed. When he tried to get up his back legs gave way. He fell again. Then he began to fit. In a few short minutes we had seen what the future held for our beloved dog.

This time really would be our last goodbye.

Jim rang the vet, who was out on calls but suggested that we take Ben to the surgery and he'd meet us there.

In the carpark we let Ben have a walk and he wandered about at first until he reached the wall. He edged along it, as if he couldn't see his way. When he moved from the sunshine to the shade he flinched. I think his eyesight had gone completely. He didn't know where to turn and stood shaking until I picked him up and placed him back in the boot of the car, talking to him and stroking him until the vet arrived.

He'd seen Ben a few weeks before and didn't need to examine him to see the deterioration. Our lovely little pet had lost his quality of life.

Jim and I were both crying and even the vet was upset. He had a particular affection for old dogs and had seen Benji quite frequently over the last few years. Having talked to us, confirming that we were doing what was best for Ben, the vet began preparing the injection.

I was holding my lovely little dog for the last time, my tears falling onto his coat. I thought of how Ben had always sensed how I was feeling, staying by my side if I was down, nuzzling at me with his head as if he was stroking me to give me comfort. He'd always been there for me somehow.

Now I needed to be there for him, not displaying my grief, but giving him what comfort I could in his last moments. I continued stroking him as I forced myself to stop crying and cleared my head.

Immediately my mind was invaded once again by Mark! I was extremely annoyed at the intrusion. This time when I mentally told Mark to leave, he did so and there were no further interruptions from him that day.

But now I knew without a shadow of a doubt; sensing Mark was not my creation, it was not something I was doing to myself.

Back home we didn't want to speak to anyone, or do anything, but had to let Peter know that we no longer needed dog-sitters. Jim phoned him, then Karen and Joanne. It was a tearful time for all.

Neither of us felt like going to a celebratory ball, but after a few hours it was obvious that we would just spend the rest of the day feeling miserable, mourning Ben. So we decided to go to Leeds. As our hotel was opposite the venue we could easily leave if necessary.

During the evening I was able to go outside for a cigarette and a walk when I was upset. Jim and I both enjoyed ourselves far more than we expected since there was plenty going on to keep our minds busy.

I was surprised that I slept that night. I think the drinks probably helped.

Losing Ben was extremely sad, but we've never doubted that we made the right decision. Jim and I still think of him often. We treasure many memories of the fun and laughter he brought us over the years, with his amazing character and crazy antics.

Benji

A dog full of character, mischief and fun,
Always so friendly, he loved everyone.

Head cocked to one side his face seemed to say,
"Don't you just love me?" And he'd get his way!

Cheeky little poser, head between paws,
Scruffy little mongrel, diving through doors!

A strong and feisty spirit, a terrier, strong and brave,
Always game for adventure he'd often misbehave.

Romping round with other dogs, barking at trespassing
birds,
Chasing cats and squirrels, he'd just ignore our words.

The minimum of training was all that he'd accept.
Never one for restrictions, of danger he'd no concept!

He was playful and cheeky, as everyone could see,
Bought by Jim for Karen, he attached himself to me.

Like a shadow he'd follow wherever I'd go
And whatever my feelings he just seemed to know.

He brought me comfort if I was downcast.
Loving, loyal and always steadfast.

My friend and companion through good times and bad.
You gave us such laughter. What good times we had!

CHAPTER 4
SUMMER 2008

Overwhelmed

When I saw Mark I felt that he was putting up a superficial front of being happy, but was actually worse than he had been in previous weeks. Instinct unexpectedly took over as I found myself, once again, blurting out something I hadn't intended to say.

"You've landed right back in what you were trying to escape!" I exclaimed in a harsh whisper, expressing a degree of anger which I hadn't realised I'd felt. I immediately regretted this outburst.

Mark had his back to me, in a corner, out of the breeze so he could light up. I wasn't sure if he'd heard me, so I quickly turned away and took a grip of myself. When Mark turned he gave no indication that he had heard me. We chatted and it wasn't long before I enquired, "How are you?"

"I'm OK," he replied. "How about you? Are things OK with you now?"

No! I wanted to shout, I'm fed up with you interrupting my life. But of course I didn't. Yet I didn't want to pretend either. Eventually I replied. "That's my problem!" whilst wondering why I couldn't just say I was OK too.

Stepping back he responded, "That means you're not. Look, you don't have to worry about me, I'll be fine. I've a good life ahead, a good future to look forward to. So don't worry,"

While we smoked he spoke of his plans with great enthusiasm.

As usual I told him to take care and I gave him a couple of my poems, despite being very unsure of how they'd be received. Passing him the envelope which held them I promised I wouldn't make a habit of it.

I wished his confident words had reassured me, but they hadn't. Not only did I sense he wasn't really OK, but I couldn't forget the horrible feeling I'd had when seeing the torn picture on my wardrobe door. I was certain that it was part of his future and it wasn't anything to look forward to.

On the next occasion, prior to a rehearsal, I found yet again that I began saying what I'd meant to keep to myself. I told him that I didn't think he'd been happy on the previous occasion. Not surprisingly he denied it and didn't seem offended.

Many people had arrived, but our vocal coach had been delayed, so most singers were outside enjoying the fresh air. It was a gloriously sunny, warm evening. We both spoke to others and were outside for longer than usual. I decided that I needed to have a much more light-hearted manner when speaking to Mark. Bit by bit the others went inside or drifted away to speak to other people so, with no one in earshot, I asked Mark if he fancied being exorcised!

"I don't need exorcism!"

"No, but I do," I responded, smiling, "to get rid of you!"

He gave me a wry grin and seemed to take the suggestion in the jocular manner intended. Later a number of us were outside again when Mark came out, lit up and walked away, crossing the road to be on his own. Watching him, I could tell he was disturbed about something. I doubted that this had anything to do with me.

It was only a few days later that I saw Mark again. Despite my previous gaffes I was able to approach him confidently since I knew there was a definite improvement in his demeanour that day. A marked upswing.

"I thought I should apologise if you were bothered by what I said the other day," I began.

He looked puzzled. "No. I don't know what you mean. What did you say?"

"Well I'm not going to repeat it am I?" I laughed. "Anyway, you're alright today aren't you?"

He looked even more puzzled and I repeated it as a statement, "You are *alright* today."

The puzzlement remained, deepening as his eyes widened. "Yes! But how do you know?"

It was good to know that I could sense his good emotions too, as that gave me a lift. But I couldn't answer his question. I had no more understanding now than I had at the start.

"Just sensed it," I replied with a shrug, not able to explain further.

Then I asked him about something else that I'd become aware of, "Do you sometimes get a tic in your left eye?"

It was a moment before he answered, still looking puzzled, "Yes. I have a weak left eye and it does twitch sometimes. Why?"

"Well so does mine....... now!"

It was something I'd become aware of over the previous couple of weeks and had suspected a link.

Shrugging again at the weirdness of it all, I walked away once more.

We had a long spell of good weather, ideal for the garden project, which was going well. As Barbara and Ian were both still working they were not usually there when I was gardening but obviously I did need to consult them sometimes. It was always good to have a chat about other things too, our activities, families and such like. It was through Barbara that I had joined the singing group. Both she and Ian had met Mark, but like me they didn't know him at all well. When his name came up in conversation one day it gave me the perfect opportunity to confide in them too. Again it was beneficial to talk openly without feeling judged in any way. Barbara and Ian know I might be crazy sometimes, in my own way, but clearly they didn't view my story as madness.

I could happily have gardened every day but then I wouldn't have seen much of Jim. We needed time together so we'd planned a couple of outings.

One was to Anglesey to try out the now completed, refurbished camper van. We'd intended to stay for a few days, but there the weather changed after our first night. We left the rain and returned home to the sunshine.

Another trip was to the Cheshire Show, which we'd not visited before. One of the first things we spotted was archery. It had always appealed to Jim and he'd been hoping to join a club. Unfortunately the nearest clubs to us didn't take beginners, and Jim had no experience whatsoever. Now he was able to try archery and he loved it. The people running it were extremely helpful. They advised Jim on which club to approach and who to speak to. He joined and has been a very active member ever since. I was so pleased that he had a new hobby through which he would meet new people and get out and about.

At the show there was plenty to see and do. The morning passed quickly and enjoyably, but from lunch time onwards I went downhill. First I felt a bit weepy. I told Jim it was because of Benji, though I didn't really think that was the reason, as I hadn't been thinking about the loss of our lovely dog. I could guess what (or rather who) the problem was and resented it. I didn't want it to spoil our day.

Controlling my tears I soldiered on but found I had no energy. I didn't feel ill but absolutely tired out. I hadn't done enough to warrant feeling so weary and knew once again that this feeling wasn't really mine. I explained to Jim and battled on for a short while, but before long I could barely put one foot in front of the other. We cut our visit short and headed home so I could go to bed.

I slept for about fourteen hours, which improved how I was feeling, but the respite was short-lived. I wasn't worrying. Everything should have been fine but it wasn't. I continued to have little energy or enthusiasm for anything. I was permanently tired. I forced myself to keep going, but it was if there were periods each day when I was merely going through the motions of my life. It became increasingly difficult for me to concentrate for any length of time. I didn't feel depressed, just exhausted and overwhelmed by constantly feeling an awareness of Mark. It was frustrating and I often complained about it to Jim, who had no more idea what to do than I had. So he'd give me a hug and a kiss, letting me know he was always there for me.

∞

When I next saw Mark we chatted normally for a while and then I asked, "Are you feeling very tired, like you're just on autopilot?"

"I've been on autopilot for months," was his reply, "Why?"

I had no intention of telling him of the exhaustion I had felt was from him. I had never revealed anything of the sensations I sometimes experienced when I sensed Mark. Sometimes my stomach would churn. Or a cloud might suddenly descend on me. Or my forehead, jaw and neck would tense. Other times I might feel shaky.

Ignoring his question I just answered, "Try to get some rest. You look exhausted."

Occasionally, in the past, I'd been able to ask Mark about specific times when I'd sensed how he felt. Each time his replies confirmed my intuition. Once I'd deliberately asked him about a time when I hadn't thought he was responsible for a brief change in my mood, and the feelings hadn't corresponded. Although I had only checked on a few of my feelings, they'd been enough to confirm the truth of what I sensed.

Still having no idea why I was experiencing such intuition I just had to play things by ear. This time I felt I should say no more, so I just told him to take care and once again I walked away.

After seeing that image on my wardrobe door, and feeling it related to the future, I had wondered about it a great deal. I thought I knew when it might happen, since there was only one time that I was sure I would see Mark; at a concert.

The morning of the performance dawned with blue skies and sunshine. The temperature rose until it was a blazing hot, sticky day. It was easy to feel uncomfortable, and I certainly did.

Of course it wasn't just the weather which discomforted me.

For parts of that day Mark and I would be in the same room, though nowhere near each other. As soon as I saw Mark I could tell from his body language that he was agitated. It was obvious from his hunched shoulders and general demeanour. He was sitting alone and when anyone approached to speak to him he would brighten up, but it only lasted until they moved away. He was certainly putting on a front again. Whenever we were in the same room I focussed on him if I could. As far as I could tell he just continued to play the accepted part when necessary, but otherwise appeared not to want to be there.

I went outside for a cigarette a couple of times during the afternoon, without seeing Mark. But during the interval we were the only ones outside. He was standing in the bright sunshine but I preferred to be in the shade, so didn't speak to him until he approached. I just commented on him choosing such a sunny spot. He looked hot and bothered, but didn't comment on the temperature. He responded by commenting on something which had gone wrong during the first half of the performance. Perhaps that explained why he looked bothered.

"Let it go. It's over now." I told him.

We chatted briefly and then I remembered that he'd previously mentioned a hospital appointment so asked if it had been OK.

His answer shocked me. "It was a brain scan."

I moved away a little to stub out my cigarette and give myself a moment to consider my reply. It didn't seem appropriate to ask why he'd needed a scan so I just joked, "They probably want to check that you *have* some brains!"

He gave a small laugh as he responded, "Well, I hope they find some!"

Asking when he'd get the results produced quite a different attitude. He stepped back, almost falling against the wall, and began cursing about how the specialist wasn't available because he was on holiday, and this would disrupt Mark's plans. He was so tense, clenching his hands as he spoke, his face tight.

He ranted on furiously about the inconvenience. I was thinking that he was clearly very bothered by this, as if his plans were more important than his health!

After a while Mark regained some composure, looked less tense and smiled a little as he made a joke about needing a drink, so he'd have to get back inside for a bottle of water. At least he looked better now than he had previously. I hoped that letting off a bit of steam had helped him.

During the second half of the performance, I found myself focussing on Mark at various times, my concentration wandering away from the words and tunes I had learned. I should have been singing without any difficulty. But I felt distracted and uncomfortable.

It was only sometime after I'd returned home that the penny dropped regarding my premonition. Strangely I hadn't thought about it during the day. The torn picture I'd seen weeks before did relate to something that day. I recalled that at one point I had been mentally telling him to sit in a more relaxed way and try to be still. Had I been on the opposite side of the room, viewing the scene from a different angle, I think I would have identified what I'd seen in the picture.

I'd always hoped that when that situation was over it would be the end of these strange occurrences concerning Mark. But after he'd told me about his brain scan I wasn't surprised when he was there in my mind at the start of the next day, and was a continuing presence. It wasn't a permanent presence but I sensed him intermittently throughout each day.

Even my all-time favourite occupation and stress buster, gardening, was often disrupted, as I continued to pick up on Mark's feelings if I wasn't concentrating.

I was still working on Ian and Barbara's garden. The weather continued to be very good, but the heat tired me. I needed to stop more frequently than usual. During one coffee break, I realised that I felt very nervy. I was used to feeling hot, sticky and tired but this was different. I'd been fine till I sat down. Instead of being able to relax for a few moments I felt on edge, though I hadn't had any sense of Mark nor been thinking of him. Then I realised I was chain smoking.

I do not do this! But I knew Mark sometimes did.

I stubbed out my cigarette and headed back to work only to begin pacing up and down the lawn.

I don't do that either! But, again, I knew Mark sometimes did.

I didn't seem to have any control over what I was doing. My actions were senseless. How ironic! It was obviously what I sensed that was causing me to act senselessly!

I gave up on the day's gardening and went home.

By the time I'd driven home I could see the funny side of my actions though they still unnerved me. Thankfully I didn't catch myself acting like him again!

At home I was working on a painting that I wanted to complete before classes finished for the summer break. I would often listen to music when I was painting. One afternoon I was playing a CD and singing along with some of the numbers. As I joined in with The Hollies' "He's Not Heavy (He's My Brother)" I was taken by the words as never before. So many of the lyrics seemed relevant to the situation. After that I would often play it or sing it, aloud or in my head. The message of the song provided me with another way of coping. They gave me a real boost.

My art work held my attention but as always there were interruptions whenever I wasn't concentrating. At least now they only came when I took a proper break, not whenever there was a lapse in my concentration. That was an improvement.

As I'd already discovered, I would occasionally sense when Mark was having a good day. One day I was absolutely euphoric! The day had begun as usual but at some point my spirits lifted sensationally. I felt as high as a kite.

I'd arranged to give Karen a lift to collect a computer. We were laughing and joking in the car and she commented on my exceptionally good mood. She kept reminding me to watch my speed and remarked that she'd never seen me drive like this!

I knew where we were heading but wasn't paying enough attention. As we almost passed the turn off from the motorway, Karen gave me a shout. I quickly swung the steering wheel, taking the car across the broad stretch of white diagonal lines from the inside lane to the slip road. Karen had her head in her hands as I made this late manoeuvre. In my defence I had checked my mirrors before the quick turn and knew there were no cars approaching. After we'd made the collection Karen insisted on driving us home. She felt my driving was erratic to the point of being dangerous.

This was all caused by the tremendous high I was experiencing! I was elated, over the moon, giggly, overexcited, completely carefree and frequently careless too. Not only should I not have been driving, but I probably shouldn't have been allowed out since I was clearly under the influence of something strong!

I knew what that influence was and guessed its cause, which was later confirmed. Mark had received the results of the brain scan. There was no serious problem.

What a relief!

Again I thought this might be the end of it all but again I was mistaken.

As summer progressed I had less to do. The sewing project was completed, I was doing less gardening in the heat, and both art and singing had finished for the summer.

Being less busy made me more vulnerable. Rather than my consciousness of Mark disappearing or even diminishing, I recognised that I was aware of Mark increasingly. Not only was I sensing him more often but the feelings of his depression were stronger. My sleep pattern was poor again.

Once more I struggled to keep up a pretence of normality. I tried to do things but seemed permanently distracted. Whether I began household jobs or hobbies they would be unfinished as I began something else. I just kept trying to be positive and not let it drag me down.

By this time I was writing more poetry. It had just slowly developed so that I was probably writing at least once a week. In the couple of years before this episode of my life I had maybe written half a dozen poems. And they were ones I would set out to write for a specific purpose.

Again the lines would begin with a repetitive rhythm, which would stop me sleeping and demand attention.

The subjects varied, but were all connected to this strange time, so frequently they related to my connection to Mark.

I considered what had occurred, the different feelings, my reactions and the strategies I had tried. I remembered the doubts I'd had and worrying that I was going mad. I thought of my frustrations, lack of help or information and how much I wanted this extraordinary period to come to an end.

None of this made me feel good. I had to try to stay positive. So I tried to be light hearted in using the lines and rhythms which had kept me awake.

What's Happening?

You said I wasn't crazy and that'll do for me,
But to know how you are feeling, tell me, please, how
can that be?

Surely it has some purpose, so what am I supposed
to do?
I talk to you inside my head! Can that possibly help you?

It's difficult accepting what's happening to my mind.
I've puzzled, questioned, researched, but no answer can
I find.

Keep busy, do some housework, is what I told myself.
Wash the dishes, iron those clothes, reorganise that
shelf.

It doesn't help, my mind still works - needs other
occupation.
Perhaps I need a different task, requiring concentration.

Success at last! It does the trick. I've learned to shut
you out.
But I can't concentrate for ever and it seems you wait
about.

When it's time for relaxation, there you are again.
Allowing me no time rest my overtired brain.

I've cursed and yelled to no avail, you will not leave my
head.
So I must try to learn, somehow, to live with this instead.

It complicates my life, and gives me cause to doubt,
As I'm struggling to understand what this is all about.

Maybe in some future time the purpose may be clear.
Until then I'll go on talking - although you cannot hear!

After working on rhymes I would feel better and able to sleep. I never wrote during the day. From time to time, awareness of Mark would be less intrusive. But the roller coaster ride, which had become my way of life, continued. Just like the fairground attraction the ascents and descents varied, some being steeper and quicker than others. My life just seemed to be going up and down continuously. I longed to get off this interminable ride and get my feet back on the ground.

Mark's continuing presence wore me down once more and as usual night times were the worst. I was thinking too much again and doing so when tired doesn't lend itself to rational thinking, but more to filling the head with doubts.

I recalled a conversation from years before.

In my teens I'd failed my driving test and didn't contemplate trying again for years. College, marriage, house renovation, motherhood and lack of funds had put it out of my mind. During my twenties I'd become very anxious about driving and even sitting in the driving seat would unsettle me. Just turning on lights or indicators had my stomach churning and if I had to start the engine I would shake!

Once my ex-husband began working away I realised how much easier life would be if I could drive and have my own car. Would I be able to do that? I wondered if I'd be able to overcome my nerves sufficiently. I worried that driving was something I would never be able to accomplish. Talking to a friend about it, she said, "You're over-thinking it. Stop thinking and just do it!" Such good advice. It took a couple of attempts but I eventually passed my test. Life did become easier when I got my own car but what I hadn't anticipated was how much I'd enjoy driving.

I had been over-thinking again and I'd let it get out of hand again. So I gave myself some good advice, "Go back to what works, keep some sense of control and get on with your life."

So it was back to keeping busy and paying a limited amount of attention to Mark whilst always being positive. Again it was successful to a limited extent but he continued to be a persistent problem; an absolute pest in fact.

Each day his interruptions would be more frequent than the previous day. I couldn't find a way to prevent this. I was back to thinking that maybe I was going mad and such thoughts are not conducive to wellbeing. I had enough to cope with without that, so tried to dismiss it.

Of course it was always at these times that my sleep would suffer.

Rhythms, rhymes and lines came more frequently. I had to avoid the negative aspects of the situation as much as possible. So I continued my attempts at a light-hearted approach.

Madness....... Maybe!

People sometimes say I'm mad, but in a humorous way.
And you said I wasn't crazy, so I guess I am OK.
But is it any wonder that I think I'm off my head
When replacing my own feelings, I've the sense of yours instead?

I'd prefer to live my life without this odd disruption.
And enjoy some relaxation without your interruption.

Maybe when it's over I'll know that you're OK
Maybe know the reason that your feelings come my way.
Maybe know if this strange sense is a blessing or a curse.
Maybe stop this therapy of writing silly verse!

Time passed with little respite and once again my resolve weakened. I became thoroughly fed up with the daily intrusions. I had still had no success in finding any helpful information, so still felt frustrated on that score. Most of all I was annoyed that I couldn't get enough sleep. I was used to irregular sleep patterns, but they generally change relatively quickly. Not this time.

I was finding it impossible to come up with any positivity, or find any humour it this situation. Any lines or rhymes which stuck in my head were much darker now. Composing was no longer therapeutic. I just wrote until I was exhausted. Even then, I never had enough sleep to feel refreshed.

I was permanently overtired and I didn't feel capable doing anything.

Often I didn't want to socialise and if anyone called it was a great effort for me to concentrate on what they were saying. I couldn't take it in. Sometimes I wouldn't realise when someone was speaking directly to me.

If friends or family passed comment on my strange, distracted behaviour, I would apologise and blame tiredness. All those who are close to me know that I've always had sleep problems. It was an acceptable excuse, partly true and I could hardly explain the other problem.

My confidence weakened day by day and night by night. I couldn't relax. I'd forget arrangements. I was becoming more tearful. Not every day was bad but again it was worsening. As well as being distracted more frequently, these spells were lasting longer again. I was overcome for so much of the time that I could barely recognise myself emotionally.

As it worsened there were times when I couldn't cope at home. I felt I had to escape. I would drive to the promenade and walk along there or on the beach. At first the fresh air, scenery and exercise helped, but after a few trips I found that once I had parked the tears would begin. The only fresh air would be from the open window as I sat and sobbed. It released some tension but was brief respite as the intrusions would start building again soon after my return home.

I had to find another way. I began taking a pen and pad with me and writing to get things out of my system. I wasn't writing verse. That had finished. I was just furiously putting all my thoughts on paper to rid myself of them as the tears flowed. The pages were full of scribbled notes and were very tear stained, but I'd continue until I found some relief.

Unfortunately, as before, this was never long lived.

It wasn't long before the tears would start as soon as I got into the car. I'd still drive to the prom and write until I stopped crying. There was little time to appreciate any relief as I wouldn't even reach home before the feelings were back again. Once I drove straight past our road because I was so distracted. Another time I took the route to our previous home, although we hadn't lived there for eight years and I'd never done it before. On another occasion I drove straight past my own home!

I could not continue like this.

Although I had previously decided, and begun, to tell Jim when I sensed Mark I hadn't divulged just how frequently it was happening now. But Jim knew I was struggling. Now I knew I had to tell him how bad it was getting and try to find an alternative course of action. I told him of the frequency and duration, the different emotions, my vulnerability, my inability to relax, my exhaustion, lack of concentration, and how I seemed to be losing myself as I was overwhelmed.

Jim offered to support me however he could, though neither of us had any idea how. We talked it all through and there seemed to be only one remaining course of action. I was past being able to fight it, couldn't run from it, so I just had to give in to it. I would have to let this thing run its course.

After our talk Jim would ask me how I was at various times each day. I would tell him truthfully how I was feeling at any time. By now I could seldom tell whether they were my feelings or Mark's, but at least I could be honest about the emotions. I could tell Jim if I was feeling ill tempered, sluggish, distressed or impatient. If I said I was alright Jim could trust me that I really was OK, though naturally I continued to be extremely tired. I no longer took myself off in the car, as we felt I shouldn't drive. I could generally cope if I could just be quiet. Sometimes I would cry and be unable to tell Jim why, just assuring him that it was some form of release and not distressing, which it wasn't. Maintaining a pretence had probably added to the tension. Now that I could just let my tears flow at will it was much easier. Bit by bit the tension was lessening.

I seldom wanted to go out, other than into my garden. Mostly I just sought peace. When I did see people I found conversation tiring, because of the difficulty I had concentrating. Jim was so patient, always there if I needed a hug, which was often. He'd fend off calls and visits on days when I truly could not handle seeing anyone or even speaking. He looked after me throughout the times when I was not myself. That seems the best way to describe it, for I often felt very odd and certainly not "myself" at all.

It must have been hard for Jim but he used his own way of coping, which matched my own initial strategy; lose yourself in your favourite hobby. In his case it's woodwork so he'd be in his workshop, popping in from time to time to check I was alright, give me a kiss or a hug and make a drink or a meal.

It was a difficult time to say the least. Nothing was straight forward about my life. Had I been on my own I think I would probably have become a recluse who neither ate, drank nor slept! Thankfully I had Jim to ensure I had food and drinks, even if I didn't want to eat. And he ensured that I went to bed, even if I did get up again most nights. It was Jim who'd take me out, driving somewhere rural or coastal so we could have a walk in the hope that the exercise and fresh air would help. Sometimes it did, but often our excursions would have to be cut short as I'd be agitated or fearful. I have no idea how I would have coped without Jim. I realised what a fool I'd been not to be completely open with him throughout all these long months.

I did virtually nothing and felt guilty that Jim was having to do everything, but he just wanted me to concentrate on getting better. Even if I tried to help, any job would be left unfinished. I couldn't even wash a few dishes without wandering off, distracted. Now it was impossible for me to keep busy. Everything was changing again. I would spend hours just sitting letting everything flow over me and not concentrating on anything.

Letting go like this allowed me to unwind. I didn't need to hide my tears, nor my fears. I could talk to Jim and I'd stopped worrying. As the tension lessened and I relaxed more, there were fewer tears and more sleep. I had plenty to catch up on! I'd doze during the day and sleep at night too.

I still wasn't myself but there was a definite improvement. I began to be able to identify my own feelings again. I sensed Mark at times each day but less strongly. I was no longer overwhelmed. Because I was getting more sleep I was no longer overtired. My concentration was better. I could manage a few chores. I felt I was recovering, which brought a great sense of relief.

Then things changed again!

Occasionally, just before I dropped off to sleep, something would emerge from the back of my fuzzy mind. Initially it was a nebulous form on the far horizon, maybe where the conscious touches the subconscious. I don't really know except that it seemed to come from a long way off. As it came forward it would change. I would hear sounds echoing softly and repetitively, slowly gaining strength. They would continue to resonate until my mind took up the chase, trying to capture the elusive patterns. By the time I grasped them I'd be awake, hearing, as before, words forming a rhythm. Just as before, it seemed important for me to do get up and work with them.

And so began my longest period of writing poetry.

I'd write until I felt I could sleep. Often this wasn't until after dawn, but I would sleep until I woke naturally, which meant I'd sleep all morning and sometimes into the afternoon. Although this bothered me, Jim told me not to worry about it because it didn't matter when I slept.

The writing intensified until I was working on the verses at nights and then in the daytime too. By the time I went to bed I would be exhausted and no longer awakened by sounds developing in my head, but that didn't put an end to the writing.

Days and nights became a blur as the only thing I could do was work on ideas whenever they came to mind. There seemed to be very little else that I could put my mind to. Again, when I tried to do other things I was distracted, lacked concentration, and was often tearful. The only thing which held my attention, and kept me from crying, was composing lines of poetry. Sometimes that was all there would be; a few lines, until I'd move onto a different poem as my concentration jumped from one thing to another.

I spent weeks on nothing but rhymes, rhythms, lines, metre, verses, drafting, writing, discarding or editing, revisiting and rewriting.

Jim continued to sort everything out; all the housework and me. Since we'd decided I should let things run their course, that's what I did. Jim ensured that I didn't spend too long in front of the computer, that I had some fresh air and a little exercise each day and that we went out occasionally. Without his care and consideration I think I would have become a recluse who neither ate nor slept!

During these weeks another change occurred. It centred my concentration. I found that the poems always focussed on aspects of depression. I remembered my own times of suffering that illness; spells which had varied both in depth and length, on and off, for over twenty years. I was able to recall many aspects of depression without becoming distraught. I seemed detached from the feelings which had been generated, viewing the past dispassionately for the most part.

I spent hours immersed in both my writing and my memories, recalling causes, reactions and results.

Mark was in my mind frequently as I wrote. As far as I could tell I was no longer sensing his emotions, but I doubted that he had recovered his health.

With the continuing focus on depression, eventually I was remembering recovery. Everything lightened up bit by bit, until I was writing about other things. And writing less.

Gradually I was able to leave my verses for a while and do more everyday things. I didn't completely stop writing poetry but at least I could help Jim a bit now. The balance began, and continued, moving in the right direction; less composition and more normality at last.

During the summer holidays I had another catch up with Jane. I really appreciated being able to talk to someone who understands what it is like to be aware of things regarding other people through nothing more than instinct. We could make fun of our experiences in a way that would be impossible without that understanding. We could laugh together and be flippant without being dismissive. Jane was interested in hearing the next instalment in my strange story and it helped that we could find humour in some things. Once again she gave me a better sense of perspective.

I'd taken some of my poems for her to read, as I value her opinion. As we talked about these I recall her commenting that maybe Mark was my muse!

I felt more positive after chatting to her because when I could laugh about these problems, as I did with Jane, they seemed less troublesome.

Towards the end of August the weather was still good, but that resulted in a problem experienced by many in England that summer. It was a particularly hot spell and we'd just changed from weekly to fortnightly refuse collection. I went to empty rubbish into the bin and found maggots crawling out of it. Swift attention was needed.

It was a most unpleasant job. Jim emptied the contents of the bin into bags and having wrapped them securely he headed off to the tip while I cleaned the bin.

Then we were both able to get out of our smelly clothes, shower and change and leave the rest of the cleaning for the washing machine.

But even when I was clean again I didn't feel too good. It had really got up my nose! No matter how much I blew my nose it wouldn't clear and I had a headache all around my eyes. I put it down to all the bleach and disinfectant I'd been using, plus the heat.

Next day we were meeting family for a meal out to celebrate Jim's mum's birthday. As we drove away from our house I began to feel nauseous. As a child I suffered badly with car sickness and very occasionally I still experience this. It generally passes quickly if I have the window open and don't attempt to read anything. On this occasion that didn't help so Jim found a chemist and bought me some medication and a drink. Unfortunately the tablets had no effect. The nausea persisted and my head was banging. I found it very difficult during the meal and had to go outside a few times for fresh air, keeping in the shade to avoid the sunlight. I wondered if I was getting a migraine, which happens very occasionally.

As soon as the cake had arrived and mum had blown out the candles we made our apologies for our early departure.

At home I went straight to bed and slept for hours. The following day I was much better, though not completely recovered, and the next day I just felt a little queasy and uneasy for a few hours. It was the same sort of uneasiness that I often associated with Mark. But I hadn't thought that the way I'd been feeling could have anything to do with him, since this was a physical rather than an emotional problem.

I remember telling Jim when the feeling finally lifted and I was fine. We were just heading onto the M62 for a day out, during which I would spend an hour in Halifax, singing.

I only started to wonder about this incident when we were in Halifax. Another group member told me that Mark had been in hospital for an operation to clear his sinuses. I presume that came as a result of investigations which had included the brain scan. The day of his operation was when my head was bad and it would probably have taken a couple of days for him to recover and get the anaesthetic out of his system.

Coincidence?

I wasn't sure about this coincidence. Some say that coincidences are not just chance happenings, accidents or flukes but incidents which happen at the same time for a purpose. Synchronicity. What purpose could this coincidence have?

I'd spent enough time pondering the purpose of all these happenings. I wasn't going to dwell on it further! No more investigation at the moment, though naturally I was still curious. I had now picked up on emotions, experienced a little clairvoyance and was possibly also having physical symptoms caused by someone else. That was quite enough! I wasn't going to add further frustration to the mix.

On the positive side, I no longer had to be concerned about what that picture had meant, or about Mark's health, since his operation had been successful.

It was two to three weeks before I sensed Mark again. It was certainly happening a great deal less now and I was thankful for that. This time I had no instinctive feelings regarding his health and that pleased me too. What I felt for a week or so was impatience, annoyance and frustration. Since I knew Mark was moving during this time, I put it down to that. So many problems can arise during a move that the emotions I was sensing would not be unusual. And they didn't overwhelm me so that was another improvement.

All in all, although the connection wasn't completely broken everything about it seemed to be lessening, moving in the right direction and would hopefully soon be over. That would just leave me my curiosity to contend with, for I would certainly never forget, and would always want to understand, what had been happening to me.

But for now I could stop worrying, shelve all my questions and get on with my life.

CHAPTER 5
AUTUMN 2008

Waves

Although the summer had been sunny, I hadn't! Now I was better Jim and I made plans.

Other than for our one night stay in Anglesey, we hadn't been able to use our campervan. Jim wanted to head south for Portsmouth to continue researching his ancestry. I had always wanted to visit the Eden project. We could combine the two, breaking up the long journey by stopping in the Gloucester area first, then spending a few days in Portsmouth to see Jim's relatives, whom I had never met, before continuing to Cornwall, where neither of us had been.

For our stop off in Gloucestershire we'd found a site on the internet which looked really lovely and we'd pre-booked. On arrival it was even better than expected.

The area to which we were directed had an old but well maintained, wooden gazebo in the centre, surrounded by a small garden. A stream ran along one edge of this part of the site with a raised bank and pond in the corner shaded by the woods on the far side of the water. It was beautiful and very relaxing.

I spent the first part of the following morning in the gazebo, trying to capture my beautiful surroundings in verse. I began many times but found that my initial ideas led to nothing.

Soon we were off to explore, first on foot and later in the camper, discovering a beautiful area which we really enjoyed.

It was by far the best site we'd ever visited. As the weather was glorious we decided to stay a couple of nights there.

The only downside was that neither of us slept well.

◈

We continued our travels, with the drive to Portsmouth presenting no problems. We found Jim's uncle and aunt's house without difficulty. It was lovely to meet them and some other family members, as their daughter and a couple of other relatives visited to meet us. When Jim talked about his work on ancestry they provided some snippets of information, but what Jim really needed was to look at records in the local office. Unfortunately the staff were on strike for two days so our research had be delayed. There was something Jim wanted to see in Portsmouth and we could explore the city. I'd never been before and it had changed a great deal since Jim's last visit. There was plenty to fill a couple of extra days.

It was very moving to visit the waterside war memorial and see the extensive list of casualties. We spent time reading many inscriptions before turning our attention to what Jim wanted to find. One of his relatives is amongst the fallen. Then we viewed the surrounding area with its many dedications. It was all a very emotional experience.

Further along the promenade we stopped for a much needed coffee before exploring Portsmouth.

Going up the Spinnaker was a highlight for me. Walking across the glass floor to look down far below and looking far out and around from the viewing gallery was really interesting, but not so much for Jim. One side effect of his medication is that he has developed vertigo. He was fine going up in the lift but once we were high up Jim had to keep near the centre of the floor to prevent dizziness. Fortunately, as the surrounding walls had plenty of large windows, he still had a good view of the landscape.

We visited other parts of the city and had a very enjoyable day.

Having done all our sightseeing on foot, plus the long walk back to the site, we were very much in need of a rest and a cuppa. But it was only a very short rest!

When he went to get the milk Jim noticed the fridge wasn't working properly. Before he had even finished his tea he started to investigate. The outlet had worked out of its seal and slipped back into the gap behind the fittings. Worried that fumes were now escaping into the camper Jim wanted to fix the problem. I suggested he could just turn off the gas and leave it until the morning, but he insisted he needed to repair the problem before we went to bed.

Out came the tool box. Off came the trim from between the window and work surface. Out came the work surface itself to gain access to the outlet. That led to the discovery that the pipe wasn't just free of the seal, it had slipped down into the gap behind the fittings.

In such a confined space there was little room to manoeuvre. Jim's hands were too large to fit into the small gap, which narrowed gradually from surface to floor. Would my dear husband give up trying? Oh no, not until he'd scraped skin from his knuckles, at which point he was quite happy to give up on that job. Not give up completely of course, just agree with what I'd kept suggesting; my hands are slimmer than his so it would be better for me to try.

A very disgruntled Jim went outside, ready to hold the duct in place when I lifted it.

Pushing my arm down the narrow space I could quite easily reach the pipe, but there wasn't enough space to get my hand around it. I only succeeded in pushing the pipe further down.

"Blast!"

Having made the job more difficult I realised that I would not reach that wretched pipe now unless I was much higher above it. Standing on our small stool was little help, but I couldn't risk climbing on the now unsecured and therefore rather wobbly work surface.

Pondering this problem I reckoned that if I could spread my weight I might stand a chance. Well..... maybe! I must stress that my weight is not inconsiderable and my overall size is above average. I've never had a svelte figure, I'm 5 foot 9 inches tall and far from agile. But when needs must you just have to go for it, don't you? Jim came in to help me. With one hand he held the counter top so that it wouldn't slide. I hoisted myself up with one foot on the stool. My body, helped into place by Jim's other hand, was splayed out across the top. It took a while to get me in a position which allowed me to move a little without Jim's support. And without danger of collapse.

If we hadn't been so tired and frustrated I think we'd both have been shaking with laughter at my ludicrous position, but at the time it was no laughing matter.

Jim went back to the outlet once I found I could reach the pipe. But I couldn't grip it. Blast again!

There was only sufficient room to get my fingers down one side of the wretched pipe. After a great deal of wriggling I managed to get my fingers inside the tube and grip it with my thumb. Now I just had to raise it up to the outlet. I tried a quick lift, but dropped it. I tried a slow, careful lift, but dropped it. I tried changing position, but dropped it. I tried to grip it between two fingers and I certainly felt like showing it two fingers, particularly when I dropped it yet again.

By now I was saying a great deal more than blast!

I gave up balancing on the stool and lay across the top, my position even more precarious than before! But whatever I tried I couldn't keep a grip on that stupid pipe. So then I pushed both my arms into the gap to enable me to use both hands and get fingers either side. Guess what? I was bound to drop it when I couldn't see what I was doing because my arms were an obstruction!

My patience finally gave out. Struggling to stand upright again I told Jim I couldn't do it. He came back inside hoping that he could perhaps get a grip of the pipe if I raised it sufficiently. I clambered back up but I don't need to tell you what happened!

There had to be another way. We needed to be able to hook it somehow. I contrived a hook from a coat hanger. At last I managed to raise the pipe, then grasp it and hold it in place.

Success!

But that was only part one of the problem.

Jim couldn't get the edge of the pipe into the outlet. After all our attempts to grasp it the end of the pipe had been flattened slightly and wouldn't fit into the opening.

It had been increasingly frustrating and continued to be so! No matter how many times I suggested abandoning the work Jim was determined not to be beaten. Our hands were scratched and bruised. We were both tired and had headaches.

I had had more than enough. I was fuming that my husband was being so stubborn. It was now after 10pm, more than 3 hours since we'd begun. I was thoroughly fed up and my temper was fraying. I went outside for a cigarette and stomped away from the campervan.

Soon I reached the hedge bordering the site where I stopped to finish my cigarette, looking towards the greenery because it kept my back to the camper van and Jim.

From the foliage a face appeared, a bodiless Cheshire cat of a face, laughing gleefully!

"Don't laugh at me." I shouted at Mark, "Don't you dare laugh at me!"

I was in no mood for this. I was furious. My hands were scraped and scratched and my back was sore. I had no patience left and was too tired. I was on the point of tears as I turned away. I lit another cigarette and was striding back towards the camper before I really took it in. The realisation stopped me in my tracks.

I'd just shouted at a hedge!

Suddenly I was laughing at myself.

Laughter, in my opinion, is the best release for tension so it calmed me down and I went back to the camper. Jim had cleared up, turned off the gas supply for the fridge and made a drink.

I didn't tell him about the incident as I doubted he'd have seen the funny side of it. All he needed was rest.

We went to bed but I didn't sleep well, which didn't surprise me, but Jim didn't have a good night either.

Next day we went for parts, Jim fixed the fridge and in the afternoon we walked along the beach, enjoying the glorious weather. After both having slept badly we had an early night but again neither of us slept well.

The following day was interesting as we researched the information Jim wanted about his ancestry and then had a lovely lunch outside the community run café.

The evening was spent saying goodbye to his relatives.

We'd planned to head for Cornwall next but curtailed our holiday. After a few nights in the camper it had become obvious that Jim was now suffering another side effect from his tablets: claustrophobia.

We headed for home and I had plenty of time to think as we travelled. I had been so glad that my awareness of Mark was fading but now there was this new phenomenon! Was it ever going to stop? Every time I thought things were getting better something would happen to throw me again! I wanted to know what was happening to me. What did it all mean? Being overtired I began over-thinking and worrying again. Fortunately I realised this and managed to stop myself.

Listening to the radio I dozed off and the short sleep revived my spirits. I decided that this latest episode was not something I should worry about. Although it had initially annoyed me, that was more because of the way I'd been feeling anyway. Really, what I had seen was more playful than sinister. And it had made me laugh which had then released my tension. Not something to cause anxiety. A reason to be grateful.

All the same, I would have preferred it if Mark had stayed away. It was almost twelve months since that first glance had stirred my intuition. How much was anyone supposed to cope with? And just what was it that I was coping with anyway?

No more conjecture or worrying. Things had been improving so stick with that.

After a few days settling back home and sleeping well, Jim checked everything on the camper and we put it up for sale. It didn't take long to sell and was bought by a lovely couple who came with their two children. Jim told them about the work he'd done, including the recent repairs. They had been looking for an old camper and ours was their dream find. I can still picture them driving it off, full of smiles and excitement. I hope they had plenty of enjoyment and fun during their travels.

⊙∽⊚

It wasn't long before I had another strange experience!

It began one night as I was sound asleep. At first it seemed I was having an extremely vivid dream and I can't identify at which point I woke.

I was lying flat on my back, arms by my sides, observing a huge wave, which was building beyond the end of the bed. It was as if I was at the edge of an ocean, yet I could see I was in bed. I was aware of the mattress supporting my body and the pillows beneath my head, though I could feel nothing.

My eyes became transfixed on the giant mass of water. Its power was immense. And it was rising ever higher as it crept towards me.

Everything was in slow motion. I could see each brilliant white splash above the crest as the wave began to break, the ever changing shape of the swell during its approach, and the variation of colour and form as I looked down the arc of the breaker to the dark, dangerous water beneath.

I was helpless. I couldn't move, except for shaking with fear. I was sweating profusely and my face was awash with tears. I couldn't speak. I couldn't breathe. I could only lie there, silent and paralysed.

The breaker was cresting higher and higher, more of its bright, white spume breaking above as it inched inexorably forward. I knew that the underlying mass of surging water, approaching so slowly, would eventually engulf me.

I was gripped by sheer terror!

The slow, inevitable progress continued as I remained trapped beneath its arc. Unable to close my eyes I watched in numb and silent horror as this giant roller cascaded over my head, roaring painfully in my ears.

I heard it pound the shore above my head. Now I could no longer see. Though I could still feel nothing physically, emotionally I was a wreck.

But once the wave had struck the surface I was suddenly able to breathe.

I gasped and immediately things changed.

The roar was replaced by the rippling of the tide as sand and tiny pebbles shifted in the shallow, undulating surf. My sweating, shaking and crying stopped. As the water ebbed beyond my head, my fear receded. I became completely calm; gently bathed in comforting warmth and light, with the greatest feeling of peace that I have ever experienced.

As the whole of my body was being relaxed by the bubbling surf it felt as if my entire being was being cleansed.

Next another roller began to build. Fear returned again as the slow motion action was repeated. Again I was shaking, sobbing, wet with perspiration and unable to move. Again the breaker rose above me, roaring as it pounded beyond my head. Again everything changed when I gasped for breath. Again I became serene and at peace as the water receded.

This whole process was repeated over and over again but with each repetition I was less afraid. Eventually I could lie watching the water travel from my feet to my head without any change to my breathing. I was in awe of the power it held but no longer afraid. The roar no longer hurt my ears and I was no longer sweating or crying as I waited to welcome what I knew would follow. Each time the tide ebbed I returned to a state of tranquillity. That impact never weakened.

I have no idea how long this continued or how many times I was engulfed, but when the final wave receded it left me with a great and beautiful sense of peace, harmony and freedom.

I slept soundly.

Jim had slept like a log, unaware of anything unusual until I told him next morning. I was still feeling peaceful and calm and felt as if something had left me.

We agreed that this might truly be the end of my unusual experiences.

It was not the end but certainly the beginning of the end.

The sense of Mark still interrupted my days but less frequently and more briefly than before. When he did, it was no longer disturbing in any way. I could distinguish my own feelings from his, so it was easy to differentiate between intuition and thought.

Gradually the experiences became shorter and less frequent. I still needed quiet times alone but now these were for me to adjust to the way I was currently feeling. It was strange to be so untroubled, unburdened, free.

Normality felt odd!

I guess I needed time to appreciate just being *me* at last.

That didn't stop me thinking about Mark and for some reason I felt I should let him know it was over, although I really didn't think that was necessary. It was just that destroying palpable evidence of the episode seemed like a symbolic gesture of completion. I reasoned, though in hindsight it was without much logic, that since it was all to do with Mark anyway, he should have a part in finishing it. And I wanted to do as much as possible to ensure it was over, because I didn't want it back!

So I wrote to Mark again, enclosing print outs of my poems complete with scribbled notes. I explained I wasn't sending them because I wanted him to read them, though he was free to do so if he wished. What I requested was for him to shred them.

Having anticipated endings before, and been proved wrong, it was a week or so before I began to feel confident that this unusual episode of events really was at an end.

It was such a relief after so many months.

I looked forward to getting my life back on an even keel, but I suppose I was over-optimistic to expect a simple return to normality. Unfortunately there were repercussions.

It wasn't long before I realised that I was now supersensitive. So many things touched my emotions.

I had been sensitive and a softie since childhood, easily upset and over-emotional. My children used to tease me about it when they were little but when he was a teenager it used to exasperate Peter. Perhaps his reaction was the reason I toughened up and stopped over-reacting. Maybe it came through the counselling or because I have a much more stable, secure and happy life with Jim. Whatever the reason I was no longer used to being reduced to tears by emotional responses.

But now I was more sensitive than I had ever been.

If news was sad, even though not concerning me, I would be disproportionally upset. Any beautiful sights made me misty eyed at least, whilst kind words, thoughts or deeds resulted in tears.

Jim and I would laugh at how much of a softy I was becoming! These times weren't distressing but could be a little embarrassing.

On a visit to Liverpool cathedral with Jim, somebody began playing the magnificent organ. As the music filled the building I was overcome by the beautiful sound. Tears poured down my cheeks, dripping from my chin. I was powerless to stop them and went through numerous tissues mopping my face.

After having cut short our earlier camper trip we decided to go to Cornwall for a week in October. We had a lovely holiday sightseeing and saw many beautiful places, which didn't reduce me to tears, but visiting the Eden Project did have that effect. Seeing pictures of how the area had been, then viewing what had been achieved had me crying. I was so glad it was raining because it provided a legitimate reason for wiping my face of both raindrops and teardrops. Fortunately both the rain and the tears stopped before long.

Later that day, still exploring the domes of the project, I received a call from Joanne, who had bought us the tickets. I couldn't speak to my daughter properly as I had such a lump in my throat. It was such a lovely, thoughtful gift! When I did manage to speak my words came out with more tears. I had to leave the dome and avoid everyone until I stopped crying.

A couple of days before we left Cornwall I sensed Mark again! The connection was clearly not completely broken, but it had been unused for a few weeks. I was quite pragmatic about it at first, although feeling frustration is not really welcome. Particularly when you're holidaying in a beautiful place and the weather is glorious. Anyway, it didn't last for long so it didn't worry me. What I hadn't anticipated was the return of his growing frustration a few hours later and again later that day and then the following one, which was when we were returning home! I was back to sensing him a great deal more frequently and with increasing intensity, which continued throughout our journey home. It bothered me a great deal, but I suppose the one positive thing was that it prevented me from becoming tearful!

As we approached home it gradually subsided and finally finished. It was the longest spell of sensing Mark for months, and the strongest too, but at last it had ended.

Then I was back to being supersensitive!

Matters came to a head when I was practising for a Remembrance Day concert. One of the pieces we were learning was a medley of wartime songs. When I began crying my eyes out because of the poor little rabbit that had to run, run, run to escape the farmer's gun, I knew this was truly ridiculous.

Thank goodness I was only practising at home and not with the rest of the company.

Clearly I needed help. I saw my doctor and babbled out the whole story through tears. She listened without interrupting or asking any questions, just handing me tissues, until I had finished talking. Still snivelling into a tissue, I didn't really take in her first response.

"All emotion is energy and you need to be more grounded."

It was't really a medical problem so she offered to refer me to someone who might be able to help, but she wasn't sure my problem fell into any category that they could help with so I would have to wait for them to phone me.

Meanwhile she suggested I went back on antidepressants. I'd been so pleased to be able to live without them since retirement, but willingly agreed to anything which might help get me back to normal.

Back home, after telling Jim what had happened during my appointment, I began to think of what the doctor had said about emotion being energy. I had never thought about that before. I'd considered energy as something physical whilst emotions were just feelings. I'd never made the connection between the two.

The more I thought about it the more I realized how powerful emotional energy can be.

It all became so obvious that I could hardly believe I'd never registered this before.

Entertainment depends for its success on the audience's emotional involvement. Whether it's comedy, music, romance, tragedy or horror, it relies on building and communicating feelings. The emotion spreads from performer to spectator and the atmosphere changes. It's a conscious use of emotional energy.

Sometimes emotional energy is not communicated deliberately. You can sense the excitement created by big events. Think of a major accident or an international problem, a royal wedding, the Olympic Games, football's world cup. The air becomes charged with such a range of feelings that it's almost impossible not to be affected, even without being involved, near or even interested.

Considering much smaller occurrences, who has not been moved to respond when people are laughing uncontrollably? It's infectious. Without even knowing what was so funny in the first place, we begin smiling, chuckling, giggling, and joining in the hilarity. Sometimes it can take a determined effort to regain composure. The power of the energy draws you in.

Seeing a baby smile generates smiles all around.

When there's love in the air it spreads happiness.

It's possible to be aware of emotional energy without any obvious indication of its source. Without knowing of any problem, you may walk into a room and feel as if you could cut the air with a knife, because the atmosphere is so thick with tension. Even though there is no visible indication of anything being wrong, you can sense it.

We are all subject to the effects of emotional energy because it is all around us. It is created by everyone. Since we are all experiencing feelings of some kind it's an energy that is always being generated, is ever present and constantly changing. It builds and spreads, touching us all, with some people being more affected than others.

All manner of emotions can be transmitted and received both consciously and subconsciously. If it is felt strongly enough emotional energy can have amazing consequences, as I had discovered.

With the variety of emotions I had experienced in the preceding year it was no wonder that I had been extremely affected. I was a little closer to understanding what had been happening to me.

I now understood the science of it, but that didn't explain how I could be affected by somebody when they were miles away. And it didn't explain the initial cause, the transmission of such a powerful feeling from that first glance, when there had been no prior indication of any problem.

I still had many questions and was back to research. All the information I found concerning emotional energy dealt with how to cope with your own overload. It made no mention of being affected by the emotional energy of others.

Now my priority was to get better. The medication helped calm me so I was not so touchy. I only sensed Mark occasionally and never so strongly or frequently as the Cornwall episode so I was able to handle it, but I still felt vulnerable.

I didn't receive a phone call from my doctor's referral so realized that the medical profession viewed my experiences as something beyond their jurisdiction, which I quite understood.

Having done little during the height of summer, during the autumn I had been working again on Ian and Barbara's garden. One day Ian wasn't at work and before I left we chatted over coffee. Since he already knew about the various problems I'd been having since I first began sensing Mark, Ian enquired how I was now. I brought him up to date and told him that I thought it would finally come to an end fairly soon.

Ian remarked, "You must have had a great sense of empathy towards him."

I couldn't believe that this had escaped my realisation. I had typed so many words and phrases into the search engine but never once had I thought of empathy! How could I have missed that?

Now I had a new path to search and as soon as I reached home I was on the computer.

EUREKA!

Although I understood what empathy was, I had never heard of an "empath," someone who can have such a degree of empathy that they have more than just an understanding of the feelings of other people. They can actually absorb the emotions so they also experience them!

I read all the information I could find. That wasn't such a time-consuming task because at that time there was relatively little available. It took far more time to find the information than to read it!

At last I knew I was not alone!

It lifted my spirits and I laughed with joy.

Now I had answers and had some understanding, although I knew it would take some time to fully comprehend all the implications of my find. And it would take further research to discover what could help.

The description of an empath fitted me so well that I had no doubts.

I was surprised to see that being an empath is described as being both a curse and a blessing since I was sure I had used both these descriptions in a poem already. I checked and found it, looked at other pieces I'd written, and then composed a sequel to one of them.

Who is the Impossible Creature?

Now I've solved the puzzle so I'm feeling satisfied.
The answer was so simple! Why was I mystified?

With help, I opened all the clues, even those I'd feared,
So the jingle's finally ended. The itches have disappeared.

Now I know the impossible creature so I must think and see this through
For I've made an identification: that creature is me, not you!

Not impossible but unusual, certainly odd but not mad.
It's a relief to know the answer after the curious times I've had!

So much of what I read about empaths fitted me. The information I collected helped me understand the strange events of the past twelve months. It also had a bearing on some things from the past too.

Now I understood why people would often think that I knew more about certain things or people than they did, even though they'd had the same information and opportunities. It had often puzzled me.

It explained why, when I had difficulties, other people did not respond to me in the same way as I would to them and their troubles. I had often wondered how it was that I could always find time for them, but often they would be too busy to help me. When I was much younger I felt that I was somehow unworthy because of this.

It all made me wonder how much of my past had been influenced, for better or worse.

Empaths were described as being spiritually aware so presumably that explained the psychic events. And apparently it is generally inherited.

It made me consider many things.

Being a good listener is one of the traits of an empath. I have a reputation as a chatterbox and after a long conversation people would sometimes say, "Well, I must get on. You've kept me talking for ages!" always implying that it was me chattering away. But frequently I would know that actually I had said little whilst they had indeed been talking for ages!

Empaths can attract people who recognise their compassion. It is all do to with generating and receiving those energy waves.

My mum would often come back from an outing having heard someone's life story! I find the same.

Sitting with Jim on a train one day the lady sitting opposite me began talking about her shopping trip, but went on to reveal the breakdown of her marriage, the difficulties experienced by both her and her husband, and various details about their past, both together and apart. I doubt she intended to reveal such information when our conversation began.

I related this to a friend some time later and she said, "I hate it when people do that!"

"Oh I don't mind," I replied. "Sometimes people just need to get things off their chest."

Picking up her glass of wine and signaling me to do the same, my friend led me out into her garden. Once we were sitting in a secluded spot she poured out her heart. We'd been close friends for decades, there for each other through all sorts of difficulties, yet she had never spoken like this before. Tears soaked her face as she revealed secrets she'd kept hidden for years, from before we had even met and onwards. She sobbed as she begged me never to tell anyone, never to reveal these things, even to her husband or mine.

As she continued she gradually calmed down and it became obvious that a great weight had been lifted from her. We were able to return inside, to our husbands, laughing and smiling as usual.

She had clearly been needing to get things off her chest for some time, though why she hadn't unburdened herself to me previously I'll never know. Maybe the energy from both parties has to pair in some way. Perhaps the timing has to be right. Synchronicity?

One of the traits of an empath is increased sensitivity. As I have already said, I was an over-sensitive child and although the intervening years had toughened me up there were still times when I feel like crying, but the odd thing is that on some occasions I have no idea why I should feel that way.

When Jane and I had been teaching together she once said I was a sponge, which horrified me at first because I thought she meant I was a scrounge, sponging from other people.

The Sponge

When first I was likened to a sponge I found the
thought alarming,
'Til my friend explained the analogy; she found my
presence calming.
It seemed whenever I entered a room I absorbed any
stress and tension.
I hadn't been aware of this and it hadn't been my
intention.

I've always been quite sensitive and often found tears
would flow
Without being aware of the reason, but maybe now I
know.
If indeed I am absorbent then perhaps when I cry
It's just a simple means of release...
.... squeezing the soggy sponge dry.

Although I had identified myself as an empath,
it took a lot more trawling to discover anything
that could help me. I managed, eventually, to
find suggestions for coping and what might be
helpful to protect an empath from becoming
overwhelmed, as I had been.

Some of the recommendations were too outlandish
for me but there were others which I would certainly
explore.

My doctor was right, I needed to be grounded. I had been affected by such a variety of emotional energy that it was if I'd been high in the sky and needed something to bring me down to earth and stay there! At least for most of the time. I simply had to find what I would feel most comfortable with.

One article I read mentioned Reiki. I'd had a short session of this years before, been fascinated by how it was done and marveled at the result. The suggestion was not just for Reiki as a treatment but also recommended training. Since I knew this was something which would interest me, I began investigating.

Although Reiki can be given by somebody who has had the earlier stages of training, only a Master can train others. So I set about finding who was in my area.

I found a number of websites and addresses locally and then investigated further. I began by visiting shops but none seemed to sit right with me. One day, as I bent down by the front door to pick up a local free magazine, I thought, "There'll be something in this for me."

Sure enough there was an advert mentioning Reiki.

When I read the information on the website it just felt right. There were a number of options available, not just Reiki but a range of help regarding wellbeing. I rang, explained briefly why I was seeking help and made an appointment for an introductory chat.

It's important to feel at ease with, and have confidence in, whoever is treating you in whatever field and I felt this immediately with Rachel. Because I was on medication she wanted approval from my doctor, who was pleased to know I had found help and willingly agreed. I have been visiting Rachel ever since for training and regular sessions of Reiki. I've also benefitted from her well-being sessions too and I am extremely grateful for all the help and guidance she has provided.

Around this time I receive more help, which I hadn't sought but for which I am eternally thankful.

I have mentioned that I'd had back trouble. It had been ongoing for over fifteen years, since the morning when my back had just given way as I washed my face. I dropped until I was hanging over the washbasin for support. I needed help to move.

Nothing specific was diagnosed.

I had physiotherapy, learned different ways of bending and lifting, did exercises and changed the way I went about things both at home and at school. I learned to bend differently and lift differently. I didn't overload myself and I asked for help more often than previously. If I couldn't walk up the stairs I went on all fours. I rolled out of bed each morning. It would take roughly an hour of sitting upright until I could move about easily. Instead of reaching down to the floor, I brought my foot up to put on socks and shoes. I organised my teaching differently so I wasn't bending down over low desks too much.

I adapted. These and other changes enabled me to carry on normally providing I was careful.

Over the years my back had given way again on three or four occasions, as the result of doing simple tasks: moving a chair, opening a drawer, picking up a piece of paper. Each time it happened I would be unable to straighten my back and when I began to walk it would worsen so that the upper part of my body would bend forwards with my head tilted towards the floor. And each time was worse than before, more painful and more incapacitating. After each episode I would have to take even more care. On the last occasion, after the excruciating pain of getting in and out of a car, I had reached home, crawled slowly and very painfully upstairs and when I found I couldn't get into bed, I lay on the floor.

I was still there when the doctor arrived and, unable to get up, I ended up sleeping on the floor. Luckily it was only for one night as heavy pain killers enabled me to move the following day.

I was scared of what would happen if my back ever gave way again.

I was always being warned by friends and family, "Mind your back!" but they didn't really need to tell me as I knew I had to be extra careful now. I would always take a moment to check that my body could cope with what I was about to do, particularly when bending, since that seemed to be the cause of the problem. I just had to monitor how my spine reacted to movement. I would ensure that my back was comfortable before I began and stop when it became uncomfortable.

I think this became instinctive after a while: like second nature.

I felt it was necessary to stay as mobile as possible and found I could manage this way. I could even continue gardening, surprisingly to the extent of digging. It just took awareness, care, and attention. Whatever I was doing I kept changing position regularly, to prevent any over-straining. And I would have frequent breaks, to stand and stretch my spine or sit with my back supported. I followed the indications from my body.

Now I had an indication of another change as I sensed something happening to my back, though there was no sensation there.

Again this experience happened during the night, as I woke once more to a huge wave building from beyond the end of the bed. In the manner of the previous time it slowly approached as I sweated profusely, silently sobbed and shook with fear, unable to move or breathe.

Because of the previous occurrence I was not quite so terrified this time, but nonetheless it was frightening at the start. I was so relieved when the roller broke somewhere beyond my head and I could breathe once again and be bathed in the beautiful, warming sense of peace as the spent wave ebbed away.

The pattern repeated with my fear subsiding more each time. The process was shorter lived than before and it was probably about half way through, as the water was flowing back around my body, that I knew something was happening to my back. There was no feeling attached to this, I just knew instinctively and certainly.

The waves reduced in strength until the repetitions ceased and I slept soundly.

When I awoke I could tell immediately that my back was different. It felt easier, freer and more flexible than it had for years. I knew I didn't have to roll out of bed, but I couldn't remember how to get up any other way!

I was cautious at first, because I didn't want to take any risks. But gradually I knew that whatever the problem had been, it had now gone.

This was wonderful!

Actually I felt it was better than that: it was miraculous!

CHAPTER 6
FROM WINTER 2008/9

Moving On

Life was good!

After twelve months of upheavals I was finally back on an even keel. I had some understanding of what had been happening, I seldom had any awareness of Mark, I was no longer supersensitive and I was generally sleeping better. This was what I had longed for! And now there was the extra bonus of being freed from my back problem.

Discovering that I was an empath had been an enlightenment. Although I hadn't found anyone with similar experiences the information was sufficient for me to identify fully.

I could relate very well to the description of it being both a curse and a blessing. I'd certainly felt as if I'd been cursed for many months but the blessing far outweighed that. I had been freed from a problem which had lasted, not just for many months, but for many years!

It wasn't until much later that I realised that I had changed in another way too. I shall never know whether this was through the long months of strange experiences, those enormous, cleansing waves or the help I received from Rachel; Reiki treatments, her training or the well-being sessions. Possibly it was a combination of them all, whatever the cause, I no longer worry!

It took some time to acknowledge this change. Worrying is so pointless. I'd always known that but the knowledge hadn't helped. Being aware that worry is no help to anyone doesn't stop you doing it.

It was as if another burden had been lifted from my shoulders.

Throughout my life I had been a worrier. Years ago Jim described me as a "worrier-warrior" because he said I was a fighter too. Now I am no longer a worrier and am far less tense. Naturally I still feel concern when problems arise, but now I don't think of all the possible catastrophes which might occur. I don't dwell on negatives and fret as I used to.

It's a great relief.

That December I celebrated my 60th birthday. We hired a hall with a bar and I made the invitations. The girls organised everything else, plenty of lovely food, a scrumptious cake and all the decorations. There were many of the usual balloons and banners but personal items too: loads of family photographs from down the years, which attracted a lot of attention, many memories and a variety of comments. A book large enough for everyone to write a personal message is one of my treasures.

I received a great many lovely presents and cards. Later I mounted all the cards in a book and wrote a long poem which refers to each present.

A couple of the guys I had worked with are in a group and as my birthday present they played for most of the night.

Without my back pain I was able to dance again, something I hadn't managed in years. I had tried on occasions, usually having to sit down before the song finished. Now I could dance and really enjoy myself.

Surrounded by my friends and family I had a great night.

As I said at the time, I might have my bus pass and officially be an OAP but that night I felt like a VIP!

I also had very enjoyable Christmas. I love decorating the house and tree with my grandchildren. Having collected a great many decorations over the years it can take some time and bring back many happy memories. On the day we usually manage to see all our close family. And as a foodie I love Christmas dinner, particularly as Jim does it all, from shopping to preparing to cooking. All I have to do is the washing up. If we haven't managed to see everyone there'll be visiting on Boxing Day too, though usually that is spent on recovery.

In the New Year I was back at the doctor's for a follow up appointment. How different that was from my last visit!

I wasn't the same person as the snivelling wreck she had seen three months previously. There were so many improvements to tell her about, as well as explaining that I had eventually found the reason for my strong intuitive sense.

I was able to come off the antidepressants, which pleased me, but the greatest pleasure came from my doctor's words.

"I'm so proud of you!" she told me. "There are not many people who can heal themselves the way you have. I know that you've had Reiki, but it is still *you* who have done this and don't let anyone ever tell you otherwise."

We hugged and I left the surgery feeling ten foot tall.

I didn't see Mark until the spring, when he still didn't look well but I could only judge from his appearance as I was no longer picking up on his emotions.

That all seemed to be over.

I was advised that if it ever happened to me again I should embrace it. I just needed to keep myself grounded and had learned successful ways of doing this.

It was months before I was aware of picking up on emotions that weren't mine and I wasn't sure to whom they might be connected. There were two such occasions, both very brief.

One Friday night I was sitting up in bed reading when I had a couple of seconds of feeling dizzy and pretty rotten. I knew it wasn't me and commented to Jim that something unpleasant had just happened to somebody.

The following Tuesday, at 7 o'clock in the evening I experienced a very uplifting feeling, which I also mentioned to Jim.

There were a couple of people whom I'd been thinking of a great deal around that time so wondered if it was either of them. But it turned out to be Mark again. On the Friday night two weeks after I'd sensed something nasty, he had a fall. It wasn't serious but he'd cut his face and had a few scratches. And it was Mark whose spirits were unexpectedly lifted at 7 o'clock the following Tuesday.

After that months would pass without sensing any emotions which weren't my own but then I'd have a brief awareness of something unusual. There was never anything more; no feeling that I should do anything, nothing which overwhelmed me for more than a couple of seconds. It no longer intruded on my life and clearly the connection was almost broken.

It was about a year before I had the chance to speak to Mark for any length of time. I told him what I had discovered and we chatted for a while.

His final remark was brief and to the point.

"If you have a gift you should use it."

A Curious Gift

My senses were in turmoil
For the feelings were not mine,
Emotions so powerful
That with mine they'd intertwine.

I lost sight of myself
As the feelings took hold.
And when they overwhelmed me
I feared what might unfold.

Discovery brought comfort
Relief and understanding:
The problems I'd been facing
Needed special handling.

The benefits brought relief
Of more than one kind
With comfort in the healing
Of both body and mind.

It is said that being an empath
Is both a blessing and a curse
And now I can appreciate
It's a curious gift to nurse.

Rhymes and Reasons

SECTION 1

How it Began

The first time I can recall writing a poem was over 25 years ago, after I met Jim. Head over heels in love, I felt I had been tossed high into the air, like a coin. I was spinning over and over, desperately hoping Jim would catch me before I crashed to the ground. I was on such an emotional high that I barely slept for nights on end. I recall sitting up in bed one night, in the early hours, scribbling rhyme to describe my feelings. When I eventually felt I might sleep, it was the crumpled paper which ended up being tossed high in the air, towards the waste paper basket. I have often regretted discarding that first poem.

It was more than 15 years before I wrote again and this time the emotions and cause were very different. The school in which I had taught for many years failed an OfSted inspection, because the data provided to the authorities was insufficient to meet the requirements of the system. We were put into "Special Measures". That night I wrote the first poem I ever shared.

Special Measures

What is the mean of self-esteem?
How do you measure pleasure?
Can you chart what's in the heart?
      I'll do the data later!

What are the units of happiness?
What is the average of care?
Can you calculate feelings?
      I'll do the data later!

Is it a bucketful of love?
Is it a cup of kindness?
How *can* I record what's important?
      I'll do the data later!

We are into special measures
And we need the measures for these.
Advisors are coming to show us how
So.......
      I'll do the data later!

Once Jim and I had made the decision that I should retire, I was under less stress than my colleagues and wanted to lift morale so I began writing poems for staff; daft rhymes and suchlike which were appropriate to the individual. But my own frustration and anger was still raw and that spilled out in other poems.

Statistics

It seems there is always something new
You demand that all the teachers do.
No wonder this profession
Has an outgoing procession!

Teaching should be for the kids
Not about charts and graphs and grids.
Some children think they can never achieve
So we find ways to make them believe.

Success may be reached down many paths,
Not just English, Science and Maths.
Our teaching aims to meet every child's need
Finding ways in which each can succeed.

Children have strengths of different kinds.
Not all have intellectual minds.
We set them challenges along each route
Acknowledging progress in any pursuit.

Our pupils receive and show respect
And as they learn they begin to accept
That life has dealt them different hands,
Individual problems, needs, demands.

We praise their efforts as they try their best,
But you judge them all by academic test.
For every child we seek an advantage,
But to you each one is just a percentage!

Whilst computing numbers, targeting, setting,
There's a basic factor you keep forgetting:
The programs should be realistic.
A child is human - *not a statistic!*

The Education System

Faster, ever faster,
Education grows,
Accelerating steadily,
The system never slows.
So take your marks
For the brain train race,
With tracking and points
To maintain pace.
Thousands of teachers
Attending courses.
Schools equipped
With new resources.
The targets are set.
Standards required.
Don't become ill
Or overtired.
The latest timetable,
Further directions,
No excuses
For missed connections.
No extra allowance
For problems to process
No excess baggage
Impeding progress.
No indications
For stop or halt,
No maintenance
To mend a fault.
To arrive on time
At the destination

Do not delay
At any station.
The Efficiency Express
Is speeding through;
A success system
For the fortunate few.

Phew!

Time

Time is of the essence,
So we all tend to rush.
Such tending isn't caring,
So the essence we will crush.

Time becomes our master,
Dictating every minute,
Diminishing our senses.
What is the sense in it?

SECTION 2

Therapy

Occasionally, after this first phase, I wrote poems for specific purposes but during the time when I was experiencing the connection to Mark I wrote, or at least started, over a hundred!

There is clearly a pattern: I write when my emotions are running high and I cannot sleep. All the emotion is generating energy so it's not surprising that I can't drop off! Working with lines of verse was therapeutic. Playing with words refocused my mind whilst using rhyme, rhythm and metre had a calming effect.

Writing provided a means of channelling the energy and thereby releasing it.

My link to Mark obviously influenced much of my poetry, to varying degrees, but some poems were purely personal and others inspired by different experiences and thoughts.

There is only a very rough order to these verses, since I wrote them so many years ago. They fall into three sections, those before, during and after the time when I was immersed in my recollections of depression.

I do remember that one verse did not follow the usual pattern. Although its focus is depression it was not written during the weeks when I was delving into my past. Whilst transferring items from a PC to a laptop I came across some unfinished lines which I had started for a colleague during my previous spell of composition. Since they were appropriate to the situation with Mark I completed them and have used these to begin this collection.

Alliterative Lines

When your world is wrought with worry
Tormented, troubled and tense
Facing the future's a formidable fear
Stress-storms strangle sense.

Depression's a dreadful, dark disease.

Self-doubt shouting stupidly
Dispirited, desperate, distressed,
Rife with regrets and recriminations
In dark depths dwell the depressed,

Deteriorating to dangerous degrees.
Depression's a dreadful, dark disease.

Success starts with a single step,
Try targeting tiny tasks.
Acknowledge any achievement.
Rest, recover, relax.

Decapitate that dark disease.
Project the powerful positive please.

Face your fears and fight them.
Wage war on worry and win.

Would You Rather----?

Would you rather run a corner shop and know each customer's face
Or manage a multi-national chain, with branches all over the place?

Do you want a job with variety, could you work on a factory floor?
Would you be happy in an office or prefer the chance to explore?

Do you seek reward for your efforts, through money, glory or fame?
Or just hope those who know you will smile when they hear your name?

Are your achievements celebrated to let the whole world know?
Or is a simple acknowledgement enough to make you glow?

Must you always be in control? If you're not, do you feel ill at ease?
Would you say you are easy-going and really quite easy to please?

Do you feel mature and sensible, not vulnerable but streetwise?
Perhaps there's a naive innocence which you cherish deep inside?

Do you favour high class hotels, frequenting the Waldorf or Ritz,
Eating from haute cuisine menus ... or just camping with fish and chips?

Would you say that you're a connoisseur of things described as fine?
Is your preference for a bottle of beer or a glass of a vintage wine?

Do you crave a busy social life, partying for pleasure,
Buzzing with the noisy crowds or do you favour much quieter leisure?

Do you rise to every challenge and enjoy trying something new
Or are routines and security essentials for you?

Few people get all they want in life, most have to compromise,
But don't ignore your own nature; that really is very unwise!

If you are forced against your will may end up feeling trapped,
But development brings changes and people can learn to adapt.

As a youngster did you imagine how your life might progress?
Think back on your achievements and consider your success.

Decide for yourself what's important; know what gives you peace of mind.
Appreciate who you really are: you're unique in the whole of mankind!

Dream Song

Hey there! Are you still dreaming?
Are you planning, plotting, scheming?
Do you dream again of what you can do?
Well I have a different dream for you.
Not of what you can do, but how you can be!

That's the dream for you, from me.

There's a key to making this dream come true
And it's held in secret, waiting for you,
You hold it yourself, it's in your heart,
That's where to look to make a start.

Take a look at yourself deep down inside
See past and present, let nothing hide.
Relinquish those parts of the past
That you need to be free of at last.

What's an illusion?
What's an intrusion?
What has value?
What is true?

The key to the dream will then be clear
As you recognise what you hold dear.
Find what you cherish and hold it tight
It must not perish, give it light.

So find the key to set yourself free.
Unlock the truth only you can see.
Become the person you want to be.

That's the dream for you, from me.

Believe and Achieve

You already know that if you believe
There's no predicting what you'll achieve.
Senses tingling, ready for fun,
Eager to work on what has to be done,
Feeling alive instead of just flat,
Wouldn't you like to recapture that?

Do you remember how good it can feel?
It came, then it went, but it was real.
Now you're feeling down at heart
As if your world has come apart,
So much doubt, so much confusion,
Disenchantment, disillusion.

Everything is tasting sour
But this is not the judgement hour.
It's just a time for taking stock,
A chance for you to stop the clock.
Slow it down, it's running fast
Move the fingers, rewind the past.

Recall how varied your life has been.
Recollect a happy scene.
Wouldn't you like to recapture that?
Feeling alive instead of flat.
Senses tingling, ready for fun,
Eager to work on what has to be done.

Use experience to make you strong.
You can't improve if nothing goes wrong.
So don't just hold your head in tears.

Don't harbour resentments, grievances, fears.
If you're stuck with troubles, anguish and pain.
Kick them out and live again!

Life's a kaleidoscope, ever changing,
Constantly moving and rearranging,
The future's uncertain, defying predictions,
Have faith and the courage of your convictions.
You already know that if you believe
There's no predicting what you'll achieve.

Count Your Blessings

During times of sorrow, anguish and distress,
You may forget your blessings, but you have them none
the less.
Although they may seem distant when trouble's at the
door
That's just the time to count them and bring them to
the fore.

Difficulties and burdens help to make us stronger
But forgetting to be thankful makes problems linger
longer.
So throw the curses overboard! Give gratitude a berth!
Count those blessings honestly and appreciate their
worth.

Give due consideration to all you have achieved,
Remember your accomplishments, recall what you've
received.
When facing each new challenge, spare some time for
thought
Of all those who have helped you and the lessons they
have taught.

Life's an endless education, one lesson supporting the
next;
As another chapter opens, don't ignore the previous
text.
View your problem clearly letting blessings dispel fear.
Empty your mind of questions so answers can appear.

Laughter

I wish there was more laughter
In our harsh and stressful world,
More happy release of emotion
Helping tensions come unfurled.

More giggling,
More guffawing,
More fun,
More letting go.

More breath-taking outpourings
As tears of laughter flow
Spreading in every direction
In an uncontrolled infection,

Our Dog

Our dog is a supervisor - nature made him a detector.
No goggles, tin hat or visor, just a self-appointed inspector.
Whenever anyone's working he'll examine what's being done
And you'll never find him shirking because his work is so much fun!
Outside, as I garden, he'll be rummaging around,
Always lending a helping paw, clawing up the ground!

Mischief twinkling in his eyes, tail wagging furiously,
Unearthing another new surprise, as busy as any bee.
Small black nose covered with soil and pink paws turning brown,
Bear witness to his diligent toil; work never gets him down!
We try to restrict his movement, for he gets in the workers' way
We've tried every single suggestion, but you can't keep instincts at bay.

He's been out in the mud again! There are paw marks everywhere!
The carpet has another stain and his coat's sticking up in the air.
We try to grab him, without success, knowing the mess he can make
As he starts to dry his coat off, by giving himself a good shake,
Followed by a furious run, round the house, up the stairs and back!

Then there's nothing like a lovely roll to complete his clean up act!

He can't keep his nose out of anything, just loving to explore.
He'll find his way around everything and gets through each closed door!
When there's nothing of interest in the home, he really doesn't care,
He'll become an escape artist and seek adventures elsewhere.
Many a telephone call we've had, from homes and shops and schools,
But there's seldom a complaint, though he's broken many rules.

He's often been fed and watered and given several treats
By those whom he's approached on his adventures round the streets.
They take him in and call us, assuring us he's fine,
Saying they've enjoyed his company and he's welcome anytime!
He's made so very many friends around our neighbourhood.
So, despite his naughtiness, he clearly makes people feel good!

Life's Learning Curves

On life's great roller coaster when you have reached each summit
Do you gradually ride the descents or very quickly plummet?

If you're an adrenaline junky always needing the next quick fix
You'll try everything on offer, hoping to learn new tricks.

But given too many challenges and forced before we're ready
To tackle another target makes most of us unsteady.

Life's a series of learning curves there's always something new.
Build on your experience to make your knowledge true.

If you haven't time to practise, what advantage are you gaining
Always jumping into action without exercise or training?

This works when we are children young enough to take the knocks
But we learn as we get older - avoid accidents and shocks.

That doesn't make life boring. Life's roller coaster is still fun,
Competence completes each stage, giving confidence to move on.

SECTION 3

The Fog

During the summer of my unusual year I stopped fighting what was happening to me and just let it run its course. It was then that I wrote day and night and the contents of my compositions also became intense. For a few weeks the subject was always depression.

The darkness of depression is different things to different people. Some may relate to the feelings I have depicted and the analogies I've used, whilst other people will have had different experiences to mine when suffering this illness.

In the story I've referred to depression as an insidious invader because that is how I view it. Churchill described it as the black dog and I can relate to that because it will "dog" you. But to me depression is more like a fog. Both increasingly diminish the senses and cause disorientation. Both dampen your spirit and enthusiasm. Both invade your space; one externally and the other internally. Both can be frightening as they deepen.

The illness is also like a fog in the way it has to disperse; it doesn't just disappear suddenly.

Everyone gets a bit down at times and this is not a problem, just a light mist! It may deepen without causing trouble. It is when the fog descends that it's time to consider some action. Medication may be all you need, but remember that the tablets will not solve the problem, just make you more able to fix it.

If you are feeling worried, distressed, nervy, and unable to think clearly, your health is at risk. Like any illness, the longer you leave it untreated the worse it will become and recovery will take longer too.

So, the deeper the fog the bigger the problem and the more help will be necessary.

Reach out and seek support.

I doubt that anyone goes through life without their physical health being compromised at times. The same applies to mental health. Treatment depends on the severity of the problem and how deep it is.

Low grade problems won't require much but ongoing or deeper problems will.

If you cut your leg it may just need a plaster, or stitches, but think of what you would expect if you had a broken leg.

You would never consider that you could mend this for yourself and you wouldn't expect a quick fix. You'd be appalled if you were just given pills for the pain.

You would know you needed professional help; that the healing process would take time and that it would be painful.

After the break had healed you would not be surprised to need physiotherapy. Even when you were discharged from hospital you would have to excersise carefully to bring all the connecting parts back to full strength. And you would have appointments for check-ups. Throughout this time you would be relying on various medical professionals.

A bone is nothing like the mind, which I think must be a great deal more complicated. But I've used this analogy because there are different levels of treatment needed, depending on the problem.

With depression there is always a problem which needs resolution.

Don't fool yourself that it will go away. Do not insist you are alright and can manage when you know that isn't the truth. Don't just carry on because it is expected of you.

Never think that you will be wasting somebody's time, that you are unworthy. I travelled that path and it was a very rocky and unpleasant track.

Professional help is required; someone who is not personally involved in any way and can identify the help you need.

Sometimes there is more than one problem. Possibly there are layers of difficulties, which need peeling away before the basic cause can be revealed. Every time a problem is solved you will naturally feel better. But that may only have peeled away the top layer.

It may be months or even years before the fog descends again. If it does, get further help. Persevere.

You deserve to be fog free!

It is all too easy to pretend that you are fine when you know you are not.

I remembered an occasion when my closest friends visited, at a time when I was experiencing another bout of depression, but hadn't yet admitted to it. I'd been fighting it unsuccessfully. I was feeling very vulnerable and didn't really want to see anyone. Although I hadn't felt sociable I thought I'd handled the visit reasonably well.

This couple were as close as family in many respects and had been very supportive, helping me in many different ways through some tough times in the past. They now lived on the other side of the country, so we didn't see them often. Usually I really looked forward to their visits, as did the children. But I just wasn't up to it on this occasion. The next time we spoke, when I told them of my depression, they were relieved. Because of the way I had behaved during their visit they had thought our friendship was at an end. Only now could they understand the situation. Apparently I had spent the whole time directing everything I said through my children. I didn't look at them properly at all and responded with a minimum of expression. I barely responded to anything they said. We hadn't had a proper conversation throughout their visit.

I would have been devastated to lose their friendship. And I'd very nearly done just that.

Not acknowledging a problem and masking it by pretence is not helpful.

I thought I had learned that lesson. Yet hadn't I retreated into pretence by not telling Jim everything from the outset? I should have known better. But don't we all do this at times, when we think it inappropriate to be really honest? Even when it's done to protect somebody, it isn't always the best way.

With depression, the deception is to protect yourself. It's a type of barrier, just one of the many ways we might react when fear triggers the basic instinct of fight or flight.

I found that as I thought of the different ways which can be deployed in fighting or fleeing from depression, many analogies came to mind. These I used in my poems and as I wrote I would sometimes recognise things I had noticed in Mark's behaviour.

He'd admitted to being on auto-pilot for months and had certainly been in need of rest. Tiredness pulls us down. I remembered feeling so tired that I didn't feel I could go on. But I had to. Instead of seeking help, I just carried on, which made things worse.

Eventually I did seek help, took medication and thought I had sorted out my difficulties. But the core of my problem hadn't been revealed. I suffered other bouts of depression over the years. And I learned to reach out for further help.

In dealing with depression it is easy to believe that you have recovered once a problem has been sorted. Naturally you will feel better, but it may just be a stage of recovery, not a complete cure.

It isn't always a straightforward process. It takes time and can be painful. You cannot rush it if you want it to be completely better.

It was a long time before I received full, appropriate help.

I saw my GP on a totally unrelated matter. As I was leaving her surgery she said, "You're not coming out of this properly. Make another appointment before you leave." I didn't know what she was talking about but did as she requested. She changed my medication and the new pills suited me much better. She also referred me for counselling. I had numerous sessions and the counsellor kept me on her file.

That meant I could return for more sessions if necessary. In all, I had four courses, of varying lengths, over a period of years.

It is essential to find the root of the problem and to keep checking until there are no more issues to be dealt with.

I'll always be grateful to my counsellor, for all that she taught me. It took a long time but eventually my problems were overcome and depression became a thing of the past.

Without that, I don't think I would have been able to recall details of my past illnesses, dispassionately. Although it was sad it was not distressing.

It was more difficult to consider the hurt which I had caused during these times, for loved ones suffer too. Wat I didn't appreciate until later was that retrieving these memories allowed the escape of vestiges of emotion which had remained trapped, something of which I was unaware. I was then able to deal with small traces of remorse, guilt, anger and suchlike. I was able to clear away the cobwebs by myself, because of all the previous help I'd been given. This catharsis came through exploring myself, as I wrote.

Throughout the weeks when I was writing about depression, I thought the need to do so was concerning Mark. I knew that it would never be possible for me to know if any of my actions ever helped him, but in retrospect I know that writing the poems helped me. Not only did it enable the releasing of those small, negative feelings from my past, but it a helped with how I was feeling at the time.

When I lost sense of myself, when I was feeling completely overwhelmed and incapable of doing anything else, remembering my past and writing poems was actually giving me a sense of self. They made me become reflective; focusing on how I had felt, how I had reacted. I had been so overwhelmed by my awareness of Mark that I had been unable to differentiate my emotions from his. But I had moved onto considering my own feelings. They may have been from the past but they were mine.

I was aware of this as I wrote. I would often be telling Mark, mentally, that I was writing about things he needed to avoid.

Empty

The well's run dry.
Naught left to give.
Too tired to try.
What good am I?
An empty shell.
A private hell.

Breaking Point

Stretch the wire
To full extension.
Tauten, tighten,
Increase tension.
Keep control.
Maintain grip.
Cannot relax.
Must not slip.

No release.
Constant stress.
Wires wearing,
Reaching excess.
System on overload.
Nerves fraught.
Mind and body
Overwrought.

Muscles twitching.
Heart racing.
Sleepless nights,
Endless pacing.
Electric atmosphere.
Emotions heightened.
Feeling bewildered,
Lost, frightened.

Breaking point imminent.
First splits appearing,
Splinters spiking,
Striking, spearing.

Slicing through stillness
Strumming their storm
Spreading vibrations
Signal alarm.

Direction uncertain,
Destination unknown,
A soundless plea
Through silence blown.

Questions

Why is there always disruption?
Where can I find peace?
Why can't people understand?
When will there be release?

Why do I feel so frightened?
Why does my body shake?
Why am I so exhausted?
How much is there to take?

Will I ever find my way again?
Why do I always feel lost?
Will I ever be well again?
Can my health afford the cost?

Why can't I stop crying?
Why have I lost hope?
Why am I such a failure?
How do other people cope?

Barriers

Closing the windows of our eyes we shield what lies within,
But shutters of concealment won't let enlightenment in.

Closed ears prevent the intrusion of further doubt and fear,
Ignoring words of comfort by simply refusing to hear.

Shrinking at the slightest touch, thinking no one can understand,
Retreating at any approaches, we ignore the helping hand.

Drawn down a negative spiral where each turn tightens the hold,
We reach a cellar of loneliness where the world is dark and cold.

No succour for this suffering soul with neither warmth nor light,
Naught to mend the broken heart or make the spirits bright.

Barriers,
Erected for protection,
Prevent the growth
Of what we seek to protect.

Invisible Armour

Wearied by life and weakened by stress
We don our armour in readiness.

Prepared for attack, we wear our defence,
No suit of chain-mail, just muscles held tense.

No hammered breastplate, but a hardened heart,
A blockade on feeling sets us apart.

No elbow length gauntlets, rugged and tough,
Just heavy handedness, awkward and rough.

No hard metal helmet encloses our head
But to self-deafened ears all sound is dead.

No visa snaps shut to shield our eyes,
Yet we become blind behind our disguise.

No shield of strong steel to deflect the blows.
Behind our pretence the conflict grows.

No heavy armour, yet such is its weight
It weakens the wearer, compounding his fate.

Animal Instincts

The wounded animal limps away seeking some
protection,
Its basic instincts now prevail. It must avoid detection.

Its safety lies in concealment, where no breeze can
carry its scent.
Not recognised by prying eyes, it lies, all energy spent.

Hurt and exhausted it has no other care,
Senses attuned to danger, alone in its secret lair.

When life's demands exhaust us, when lost in confusion
and doubt,
We are wounded creatures too and animal instincts out.

Retreat, withdraw, retire, our only chance is flight,
For battle-scarred and weary we can no longer fight.

Overwrought and anxious, exhausted and careworn,
Seeking the safety of refuge, the stressed become
withdrawn.

Secure in private sanctuary, seeking no assistance
Doubts permeate our senses, promoting our resistance.

Repelling intrusion, rejecting approaches,
Retracting from touch, suspicious of motives,

Introvert being doubting its worth.
A wounded animal gone to earth.

Hiding

I'm hiding where you'll never find me.
I'm hiding inside my own head.
You may think you can see me
But you see pretence instead.

You only see the outside,
A front, a mask, a sham.
You do not really see me.
You cannot know who I am.

I'm hiding where you'll never find me.
I'm hiding inside my own head.
In a cell of false security,
Where I'm neither living nor dead.

Neither fully awake nor sleeping,
My life is a series of dreams,
Each becoming a nightmare
For nothing is as it seems.

I'm hiding where you'll never find me.
I'm hiding inside my own head.
Inside a dungeon of deceit
Where doubts and fears are fed.

I'm lost within the intricacies
Of the labyrinth of my mind,
Where every road is a dead end
And every corner is blind.

I'm hiding where you'll never find me.
I'm hiding inside my own head.
Full of trickery and deception,
A prison that I dread.

The Robot

I'm a walking, talking robot
With many missing screws,
Loose bits forever jangling
And parts I cannot use.

I'm so run down and rusty
I stumble, trip and fall
And frequently I'm finding
That I cannot work at all.

Though programmed for feelings
My connections are haywire.
Nothing makes me happy.
There's just one thing I desire:

Just replace what's missing
So I'll function as I should,
Please reconnect emotions
Which allow me to feel good.

I know it won't be easy
To repair inside my head
So if that task's impossible
Please dismantle me instead.

Worrier-Warrior

I am a worrier.
Tension holds me tight.
I am a warrior,
With battles to fight.
Mind and body bear the scars.

Bruises hurt,
Wounds bleed.
Skin mends,
Breaks heal.
But scars remain.

Sleepless nights,
Daily grind
Black clouds.
Troubled mind
Bears scars unseen

Light dawns
On clearer skies
Welcome recovery
Pain slowly dies
Scars become history
Of a personal past.

Many obstacles overcome
Numerous battles lost or won.
Years go by, the fight goes on.

It's seldom an easy passage
From birthing bed to grave

Surviving conflict,
Struggling for release,
Fighting for freedom,
Striving for peace

The fight will continue
While life and love remain.

Healing Old Wounds

The wound that you suffered needed tending to heal
But the hurt and its depth you strove to conceal.
Denying its influence was your only goal
So you hid it from sight to maintain control.

Kept tight inside you, given no air
Ignored and rejected, the hurt rotted there.
Lick that old wound and you'll spit out the taste
Of the festering ulcer covered in haste.

Reveal it with honesty and clean it with clarity
Cleanse with forgiveness and dress it with charity.
Let the hurt surface for it's time it was gone,
Heal it completely so you can move on.

Developing the Negative

Colourless negative,
Image ill-defined,
Unfinished picture,
Base print, unrefined.

Bleak, black backdrop,
Shrouded, sketchy scene,
Shadowy, skeletal silhouette,
The negative is mean.

By reversing the values
Truth is denied,
Reality is clouded,
Honesty belied.

Enhance the picture.
Lighten the gloom.
Develop the image.
Escape the dark room.

Illuminate the character.
Reveal its truth and worth.
Expose it with colour
For positive rebirth.

The Tunnel

Swirling darkness envelopes you
In the tunnel's airless depth
As you stagger blindly onwards
Struggling for breath.

Unsure of where you're going,
Groping your way about.
Lost in a fog of misery,
Disillusionment and doubt.

In that dense mist of depression
You've lost track of time and space
But eventually the fog will lift
To reveal your rightful place.

Light shines at the end of the tunnel!
Impatient to reach the source
You charge out into sunshine,
Ignorant of its force.

Its brilliance is blinding!
You shield your eyes from strain.
Recreating that darkness
To hide a while again.

Readjust more gently.
Allow yourself time to recover.
Step more slowly from the shadows
There's a world to rediscover.

Let the welcoming light illuminate
Both the present and the past.
As its rays reveal reality
Let that enlightenment last.

SECTION 4

Into the Light

Gradually I had been shifting away from writing only about depression and was moving towards depicting recovery. I think it was probably around this time when I stopped writing night and day. In the same way that the intensity built, it now declined. I continued composing lines, sporadically, until 2009, and have written a few since.

Life

Life is a short four letter word, and one of them is F,
Though there may be cause for cursing, to obscenities
I'm deaf.
Yes, life does have its problems, worries, doubts and
fears.
But life's too short to be bitter. Don't waste the precious
years.

L is for learning, laughter, love and light,
Look for positive aspects, don't let wrong eradicate
right.
Leave losses behind you, learn from the mistakes.
Laugh at little errors, they're only life's "out- takes."

I has immense importance, though may not be ideal,
I'm an interesting individual, imperfect, yes, but real.
I become involved, I interact, don't treat me like a robot.
And I don't have all the answers; a computer I am not!

F is for finding fulfilment. Life is a web to be spun,
Fashioned from fibres of friendships, family and fun.
Frame it with forgiveness, life is complicated.
Fill it with positive feelings. Its form is not dictated.

E is the ending, giving time to reflect.
Life often brings us what we expect.
Anticipate failure and you can't succeed.
Have faith in yourself. You will find what you need.

Life Can Be Wonderful

Lack of luck's no limitation,
Invest in your own inspiration.
Face you future with fascination,
Excitement, enthusiasm, expectation.

Count your blessings.
Accept mistakes.
Nobody's life is perfect.

Believe in yourself.
Enrich your life.

Wishes can come true.
Open your mind to opportunities.
Never doubt what you can do.
Differences present new challenges.
Enjoy each changing view.
Relax and reap the rewards.
Find faith; it's inside you.
Use time and effort wisely
Life is a career to pursue.

Be Gracious in Receipt

If you get pleasure from giving
Remember, whenever you take,
Others deserve the same feeling.
It's their pleasure now at stake.

If the gift is not just what you wanted
It's rude to make that clear
Seeing only the present is selfish
If someone is being sincere.

If you are feeling unworthy,
Overwhelmed or taken aback,
Turn away from yourself, to the giver,
And give some pleasure back.

Poppies for Remembrance

Little bright red poppies worn with patriotic pride
As we humbly remember the millions who died.

Simple, modest poppies, with petals red as blood,
Small tokens of remembrance for lost brotherhood.

Remember the fallen, wherever they lie.
Brothers and comrades, too young to die.

Thank them for our freedom; we can never repay the cost
Dearly paid by many whose lives were maimed or lost.

For us they gave their future; thank them for their past.
Our peace is their legacy, long may it last.

Little bright red poppies, recognised worldwide,
Symbols of sacrifice, humility and pride.

Now I am 60

I dreaded being sixty,
Old is not a pleasant tag
Age determines the label:
Pensioner, what a drag!

My travel pass has now arrived
With my picture, so severe!
I think I look quite awful,
A real OAP I fear!

Is that really how I appear?
Into the mirror I squint
I may be wearing glasses
But there's certainly no rose tint!

I give close examination
To every wrinkle and line
And every single facial hair
To check if it's coarse or fine!

I notice bags beneath my eyes
And fat in my cheeks and chin!
If I start a diet immediately
How long will it take to be thin?

Solutions are available
For turning back the clocks
But I don't fancy a face lift
Or filling with Botox!

The lines are growing to furrows,

Eyes narrowing with a frown.
Now I've wrinkled every feature
From double chin to crown!

For goodness sake you silly woman!
Whatever did you expect?
You've had this face for sixty years.
When was it ever perfect?

Now it's laughter that wrinkles my eyes
And I see them twinkle in fun!
I've worked out what's wrong in that photo.
I think all the colours have run!

An Alphabetical of Philosophy

Achieve your potential.
Believe in yourself.
Cherish the life you have.
Draw strength from trust.
Encouragement promotes growth.
Friendships spread good feelings.
Give with generosity.
Have the courage of your convictions.
Intuition is a pathway to truth.
Judgement is not just without all the facts.
Know yourself and be true to your beliefs.
Love yourself more and you'll have more love for others.
Mistakes are human; forgive them.
Now is the only time you have, treasure it.
Open your mind and your heart.
Problems bring opportunities for learning.
Question what you doubt without doubting what you know.
Receive with pleasure and gratitude.
Share good fortune, no matter how small.
Try your best; no one should ask for more.
Understanding others helps you understand life.
Viewpoints change as your position alters.
What you think of me is your concern, not mine!
X may signify a mistake, declare your vote or send a kiss.
You are the most important person in your life.
Zero is the bottom line: the only way is up.

Home

Home is not just a known address
Where material comforts may please.
It's where I find contentment.
It's the place where I feel at ease.

My feelings define my residence
So home is the place for me
To be myself, unashamedly,
Comfortable, relaxed and free.

Home is a place of freedom,
Home is where I find peace.
Home is the safe haven,
Where emotions find release.

I feel at home by the ocean,
Hearing breaking rollers roar,
Or watching a gentle, rippling wave
Washing pebbles across the shore.

I feel at home with nature
Breathing the scent of fresh air
Feeling sunshine on my face
Or breezes ruffling my hair.

On a springtime walk in the country
I marvel at nature's rebirth.
Roofed by space's infinite sky,
This magnificent home; this Earth.

Home is a very personal place.
Its foundations are deep and strong,
Built with love and understanding.
Home is wherever I feel I belong.

Good Days and Bad

On a good day I look in the mirror quite pleased with what I see
On a bad day I groan in disbelief. Oh dear, is that really me?

On a bad day I turn from the mirror, unable to face my reflection,
Wrinkled lines, pockets of cellulite, bulges of imperfection.

On good days I count my blessings without even having to think.
On bad days I'm so ungrateful; no wonder my spirits sink.

On a good day I see my appearance as recording what's gone before;
The result of life's experiences. I'm smiling and eager for more.

Having a Laugh

I wish no harm to others, though some people I may shock;
It's just good humoured banter when I joke or tease or mock.
I prefer to look for the funny side of troubles that arise,
Though this can be annoying and at times a little unwise.
Others may disagree with me and find my way absurd.
They've a right to their opinions and rightly these are heard.
If they feel things strongly then their feelings they can air
But I don't care to scream or shout or cry or moan or swear.

I'll say my piece, and then some, since I am a chatterbox.
I'll attempt to say it calmly so the meaning isn't lost.
But even with serious subjects I'd sooner have a giggle
At inappropriate moments my lips will silently wriggle!
I'll keep them shut, not a sound will I utter,
For fear that my words will come out in a splutter!
That might cause a problem and appear unkind
Since some people are easily offended, I find.

It's not the people I laugh at but words and situations.
Life's too short for overblown, longwinded deliberations.
Laughter's an excellent medicine and makes you feel less tense.
So whenever you think I'm silly, please, have a laugh at my expense.

King Arthur and the Plights of the Unstable

It began as a mumble
When I started to stumble,
    But the meaning was unclear.

When first I did tumble
It grew to a grumble;
    Words I could almost hear.

It sounded like a plea
Regarding my sore knee.
    An unusual call for help.

Next it was my hip
Which was giving me jip,
    And the call became a yelp.

When I detected my leg swelling,
It was this which caused the yelling.
    Demanding the aid I was seeking.

As my bones were creaking,
My joints began shrieking,
    To a famous ancient king!

Now there was no doubt
As the message rang out,
    "Arth, right us!"

The Perfect Gift

Its boundaries are endless
Yet it takes up little space.
It's easily shared by others
Yet always stays in place.
It has no language barriers
Can be used at any stage
By both male and female
No matter what their age.
It needs no storage, nor repair,
Never wears out or grows old.
It's useful in or out of doors
In both warmth and cold.
It doesn't cost a fortune,
In fact it comes for free!
All it needs is freedom.
Whatever could it be?
It's such a magical present
And you have the information
Have you spotted the perfect gift?
Just use...............imagination!

Painting Love

Will I ever be able to paint love,
Now that I've taken up art?
It has so many guises
Depending on its heart.

I'd depict the love of glory and fame
With slashes of gold, red and white,
Clashes of metals, sashes and medals,
Vibrant colours, depicting the fight.

For material love of money
I'd use soulless shades of steel,
Sharp, spiny signs with angular lines.
No subtleties here to reveal.

Interpreting love of nature
Demands intricacy, refinement, care,
Stillness and movement, textures and hues
For the miracles hidden there.

I might try to capture romance
With a delicate, gentle brush,
Carefully, thoughtfully, kindly,
With a smooth and silky blush.

But what of the love of close friendship?
Neither romantic nor dependent,
Not materialistic nor overbearing,
Yet brilliantly resplendent.

Multi-coloured memories
Mixed for the expression
Of mutual trust and honesty,
Truthfulness with discretion.

The Race

We're all in the pursuit event, on the starting line at
birth.
It isn't fair, this human race, but it's mankind's life on
earth.

The course is often uneven with many a hurdle and
trap.
Some start with an advantage, others carry a handicap.
Though it's been running for centuries there is still no
plan or map
No one can number the current round, nor name the
heat or lap.

We aim for personal triumph trying to prove our worth.
It's the strangest competition, this human race on earth.

My final poem was inspired by "The Armed Man. A
Mass for Peace" by Karl Jenkins. I knew only a few
parts of this before a workshop and performance
with the singing company. I was immediately
captivated by this brilliant and very moving work
and have been fortunate in being able to participate
in a number of other performances. These lines
were written in 2009, when my long spell of writing
poetry was almost at an end.

Still

Still more fighting
Still more suffering
Still more dying
Still more war.

Down the ages, throughout the world,
Men have fought, for power,
For beliefs, for possessions,
For the glory of victory's hour.

A history of bloodshed,
Millennia of war.
The fighting continues
For man still wants more.

There cannot be peace for all mankind
Till man learns to still his restless mind
And in the stillness listens
To that still small voice within,
Whispering of peace.

Being an

Empath

My Discoveries

It was an enormous relief to discover there was such a thing as an empath! I could identify with what I found and it was a great relief to know I wasn't alone.

In the intervening 10 years a lot more information is available. The internet has many sites about empaths and there are plenty of books too.

But I think the problem which I had is one which may still apply to others: if you have never heard of *an empath* you won't know where to look for information. It is not a generally known condition. Other paranormal abilities, such as sixth sense, psychic, clairvoyance and telepathy are in most people's vocabulary even if they have little knowledge of them. "Empath" is not in the general domain.

So if my story made you wonder about yourself, or somebody you know, here is a brief description of the things you may be wondering about. They have been gleaned from my experiences and my searches, both at the time of my story and since.

I must stress that I am not an expert, nor medically qualified in any way. This is merely a layman's guide!

Definition

Empath: a person with paranormal ability to perceive the mental or emotional state of another individual.

This is a dictionary definition but I have omitted the first part (*chiefly in science-fiction*). Just because science cannot explain it does not mean it is fiction!

I didn't discover any definition all those years ago, otherwise I would have recognised myself as soon as I read it.

My identification came initially from reading of the common traits and was backed up by later research. Since then I have read of other shared attributes, so I have combined them all here.

It does not take all these characteristics to be an empath, but if many of them apply to you it becomes a possibility.

Traits of an Empath

- Often labelled too emotional or oversensitive.
- Enjoy helping others.
- A strong connection to nature.
- Having an affinity with animals.
- Very intuitive.
- An inherited trait.
- Creative and imaginative with a wide range of interests.
- Non-violent and non-aggressive.
- Naturally giving.
- Spiritually attuned.
- Good listeners.
- Loyal.
- Prone to depression.

- Can become emotionally drained by crowds
- Require time alone.
- Take longer to wind down, as ability to transition after stimulation is slower.
- Natural carers

If you recognise that you have many of these traits, you need to consider the following:

Identification

The key is to recognise the difference between your feelings and those which are common to others.

Many people are very sensitive and emotional, but with an empath it is more of a **super-sensitivity**. They may be over-sensitive to sound, light, smells or touch as well as to emotions.

Just as being empathetic is different to being sympathetic, so being an empath is different to having empathy.

When something bad befalls others you may have sympathy; feeling sorry for them. If you can identify with their problem you will feel empathy. Actually **feeling their suffering** is what defines an empath. It is very easy to be affected by the happiness of others and feel your own spirits being raised in this way, which is why identification is best done through suffering.

An empath is able to **absorb the feelings** of others.

Cause and Effect

When looking for the cause of these super-sensitivities I found two explanations. I have tried to explain them very simply.

1 Right from birth we learn through investigation and observation. We internalise the information received to make sense of the world around us.

Everything has energy and emits this through energy waves. As babies move around their energy waves meet those from other people and things. This is how we all initially begin to understand our environment and learn. The waves of energy vibrate. It is these vibrations which can be translated.

At some point, in normal development, the balance shifts from outward awareness to self-awareness. The child becomes more involved in their own identity and less devoted to all that surrounds them. This shift does not happen in the same way with empaths. Although there will be some awareness of self, they continue to be more outwardly mindful, still taking in everything from their surroundings.

Because they continue to be very observant, they become more conscious than others of all aspects of body language. Further to that, they receive information not just through sight and sound, but also through feeling.

Empaths hone their skills of understanding others through a continued awareness of emotional energy. Being attuned to the changes and nuances of this energy they develop an awareness, which goes beyond the norm, as they translate the vibrations of the energy waves.

2 Research has shown that there is a difference in the brain.

I am describing these in layman terms, as simply as I can, based on how I understood .what I read)

Having identified the cells which are responsible for compassion, scientists found that the associated mirror neurons in the brain of an empath are enlarged, with more sensitive receptors than usual.

The brain is wired differently and lacks the usual filters for emotions.

This makes an empath hyper-responsive and able to absorb the feelings of others.

Both a Blessing and a Curse

Empaths are said to have a **complete communication package.** They are natural **receivers** for the emotional energy transmitted by others. They are also very **aware** of body language, inflection and nuances in voice. Being **highly intuitive** they will instinctively know things which are not apparent to others. This awareness, together with their **natural instinct** for **helping** others, their **honesty** and **loyalty** and the liking for **solving problems,** are the reason that being an empath is described as a **blessing**. Though in my case it led to so much more.

It is also a **curse,** because this communication package can work both ways. Since empaths emit their own energy signals, they can be identified as people with whom others may communicate easily. They can become **overwhelmed** by all the emotion they receive during these communications. But, even without any verbal messages, they can be absorbing the feelings of others. In **crowds** they can be bombarded with such a variety of emotions that it makes life very difficult. This is further aggravated by their own, **over-developed sensitivities.** Empaths can feel everything emotionally, sometimes to extremes. Another problem is that they are **vulnerable** to the attention of those who prey on others, who may identify an empath as an easy **target**.

The extent of these difficulties will naturally vary, as will the results.

In my case I would often be reduced to tears but I know some empaths can be physically sick. They are commonly prone to depression and nobody can tell what other **illnesses** might ensue; not just **mental health** but **physical illness** too. As well as having anxiety or panic attacks, which may be very debilitating but can be diagnosed, they may also suffer from physical disorders which might baffle the medical profession.

Their own nature does not help. Because empaths tend to be more conscious of the needs of others, rather than themselves, they often **neglect** their own health.

They may also indulge in **over-eating** and other forms **of binging**.

Difficulties in **relationships,** due to the strong impact of emotions, can be a further problem.

Coping Strategies

The most important thing to realise is that you shouldn't concern yourself with other people's troubles to the extent that it affects you adversely.

Because empaths are more attuned to what is outside of themselves, it is easy for them to neglect what is inside, i.e. their own needs.

Become more **self-aware**. Listen to your body and respond appropriately. Learn to **put yourself first.**

Create a healthy **mental life style**. Try to be positive and **learn to love yourself**. "Loving yourself" is often used in derogatory ways, to imply that someone is self centred, arrogant and doesn't have much regard for other people. But that's when they are too egotistic. I'm talking about having **positivity** in your attitude to yourself, showing yourself the consideration you'd show others; the time, appreciation, mercy, forgiveness and understanding. This isn't selfish but common sense. If you don't take care of yourself your health will suffer, and you won't be of any help to others. Another benefit is that the more love you have, the more you will receive. So start with yourself. In your life the most important person is you!

Consider your characteristic and **appreciate who you are**. Nobody is perfect. Look at your successes not mistakes. Nobody can be good at everything, consider your achievements not shortcomings. If there is some aspect of your character which you don't like, consider how you might change it. It will be worth the effort. Be happy with yourself and your life will be happier.

A healthy **physical life style** is also very important for empaths because of their unwitting self-neglect. Naturally a healthy **diet** and **exercise** are a major part. High protein meals are recommended for centring. (More about centring later.)

Sleep and rest as much as you can; obviously this varies from person to person. I have read that empaths require ten hours sleep each night with an hour's rest during the day and breaks in between. But I presume you also have a life to lead!

Because an empath takes longer that others to transition from one state of mind to another, they cannot wind down quickly and may not get enough sleep. Try to make up for lost sleep if you can and relax whenever possible.

There are many **relaxation** techniques which are beneficial; tapes, aroma therapy, massage etc. If you can **meditate**, it is very beneficial. Find whichever methods suits you and appreciate the feeling of relaxation, letting it remove any tension, then continue to hold this good feeling.

Learn to say no. As naturally helpful people, empaths frequently agree to take on more than they should, overloading themselves so their own needs are neglected, which can result in illness.

If socialising is difficult, because you experience overload in crowds, **limit your time** on these occasions. Choose areas at the event which are away from the central crowd. You may well find it easier to be on the periphery; at one side or in a corner.

Whatever you are doing, if you are with others for a long period, ensure you have breaks. **Time-outs** in the fresh air are best.

Talking about your experiences is helpful. If there is anyone you know and trust who is open-minded and not judgmental, speak honestly and fully with them. If you are being badly affected, make sure your loved ones understand. That way they won't feel shut out and concerned, sensing a problem but unaware of its nature, which could create further problems in the future. Being an empath is not a guilty secret to hide!

Even at home you need to have **your own space**. Your family needs to understand this, to know that this is more important for you than it may be for them. **Explaining** to family may not be easy and you may find each member reacts differently.

No matter what response you receive you need to emphasise your need for **quiet times.**

There are ways to help manage being an empath and in some cases you can **use your blessings to overcome the curses.**

Avoiding conflict comes naturally to empaths, which means they are automatically avoiding negative energy though it's impossible to avoid all problems.

It's easy to be **hurt** when you are super-sensitive. Your natural talent gives you a better insight into the true feelings of others. It is important to remember that they will probably not have the same insight into you. Don't be upset if they cannot react with the same level of compassion towards you.

Try to be **open** about your feelings, to give others a better understanding. Many empaths are introverts and there's nothing wrong in that, but some hide because they fear being hurt or used. They avoid close relationships, because the levels of emotion created, on both sides, could be too much to bear.

If they had better ways of coping it could open up more possibilities for them.

It's important to **stay true to yourself**. Don't give in to the will of others just to keep the peace. If you do you may be burying resentments, filling yourself with negative energy.

Feeling overcritical of yourself is common with empaths, who will feel particularly bad if they think they've offended others. Try not to beat yourself up. We all make mistakes. The point is not to over-react and apportion blame, but to put mistakes right and fix the problem as soon as possible.

You will also need to **control all the energy** which you absorb, whether it comes from personal interactions or those beyond your control. Mood is adversely affected by picking up bad, negative energy but a beneficial effect comes from good, positive energy.

An appropriate **balance** is important for everyone who wishes to have a happy, healthy life. For an empath, who needs to avoid overload, this demands even more attention. You need to stay **centred** and **grounded.**

Centring

I've already mentioned that a **high protein diet** is said to help with centring. I am not adding anything further about that as it should be easy to find information about any type of diet.

I shall just explain, simply, why centring it is important and techniques which are recommended

If you have been overcome by picking up emotions from other people, it is easy to lose sense of yourself. It is important to rediscover that sense of self. Take time to centre your thoughts and actions on yourself, to regain control.

Breathing exercises are beneficial for many things and are simple. We frequently breathe just using the upper parts of our lungs so practice **breathing deeply**. Learning to breathe deeply should not be rushed. Do it at your own pace, with counting which suits you, so that it is easy and you don't become light-headed. This way it is easy and does not take long to master.

Feel the air filling your lower lungs by placing your hands on your abdomen and feel it **expand** as you inhale and **retract** as you exhale. Start with just a couple of breaths and increase the number each time you practice. When you can manage ten deep breaths easily you can move on to further adaptations: breathe in to the count of six and out to the same count so you are increasing your control.

Again, once this is easy you can add to it by count further, gradually increasing to a count of ten.

Another adaptation is to inhale, hold your breath, then exhale, each to the same count. With each step you should keep your **awareness** on how the movements affect you. Always remember to stop if you feel uncomfortable in any way.

The final thing you can introduce is to finish exhaling with a final puff of breathe. You probably thought you were emptying your lungs before, but we tend to hold on to a little stale air, so get rid of it!

You will now be accustomed to feeling the expansion, retention and retraction of air because you have been feeling it with your hands and you have been concentrating on your breathing.

Next move on to a **visualisation** technique, concentrating on deep breathing *without counting or holding your breath.*

As you inhale think about the air refreshing your body and visualise it spreading throughout each area. It is health-giving and good. Feel it strengthening each part of your body. It is bringing you good energy, sustaining you.

Exhaling is removing what is spent and of no further use to us. Concentrate on letting go of all the bad energy. Blow it away.

Because you have been **focused** on your own body during this time, it helps to **centre** you once more.

One of the advantages of developing this breathing exercise is that you can practice it anywhere, anytime because it can be as long or as short as you choose. You could try to incorporate it into your daily routine, using it while you are waiting for the bus or train, stuck in a traffic jam or just at the traffic lights.

Grounding

As well as centring you also need to be grounded.

Some people are referred to as being "down to earth" or "having their feet on the ground" and this implies that they are straight-forward folk who can handle what life throws at them without getting carried away by an excess of emotion. Empaths certainly need to work on that, which is why grounding is essential.

Again there is a visualization technique which you can carry out anywhere. It's all to do with **releasing unwanted energy** in a safe way. I think of it like electricity requiring earth wires for safety!

Imagine you are standing outside, on the bare earth, rooted to the ground. Your imaginary roots, or earth wires, go deep into the ground. They are the means by which you can rid yourself of any depleted, negative or excess energy. Concentrate on sending that energy deep down into the ground.

Many activities are good for both centring and grounding, enabling you to free yourself of negatives and have a better sense of yourself.

Nature and the outdoors can be very helpful. Get out into the **fresh air** and enjoy it. Give it your attention. Watch what is happening wherever you are. Notice all the different aspects of nature; the variation of forms, colours and textures. Listen to the birds or the wind or the waves.

Focus on your surroundings. At first it may not be easy and may need a little time and concentration. Once it has captured you, you will lose yourself for a while, along with your problems!

If you don't have time to take a trip to somewhere rural or coastal just go to a garden, a park or a wood. Wherever you can, allow nature's energy to wash over you.

Animals are also useful in this. Stroking or playing with animals has been shown to help relieve tension.

Expressing your **personal creativity** is another means of centring. Whatever form this takes it is good **therapy**, which can work on different levels. It gives us time for ourselves and is a source of relaxation. Being creative is a positive thing, which gives us a sense of achievement. It centres us because we are focusing on our own ideas and experiences for expression.

There are also many **holistic therapies** which are beneficial. Practices which offer a variety are easily found these days.

My preference is **Reiki**. It works on the principal of universal energy and how to channel it, so it's ideal for empaths. Just ensure that you are completely at ease with the practitioner and the surroundings.

Reiki works in a variety of ways, depending on need. I suggest that you have a course of treatments to put you into a good place. You will be able to judge for yourself how many sessions you will need, as well as being guided by your practitioner.

Taking the first stage of learning Reiki will allow you to treat yourself. You will need to be taught by a Reiki master, but treatments can be given by people who have not reached that stage. I believe you should experience Reiki first to appreciate its effect. I would advise against rushing into learning and initiation.

There are courses available which will train a number of people in the both stages one and two in just one weekend. And you don't even need to know anything about Reiki or have experienced it! I think they probably fall into the category of "if it sounds too good to be true, it probably is!"

As well as strategies to help you cope, you will also need to learn ways to shield yourself so that you can avoid picking up energy. You can learn to control your empathy and avoid an overload of emotion from others.

Protection

The most obvious way to protect yourself from negative energy is **avoidance.** If you are aware of generally feeling drained or out of sorts after spending time with a particular person, it makes sense to avoid contact if possible. They are not doing you any good!

This is also another means of managing the times when you feel unable to cope in crowds. Sometimes I have sent my apologies for not attending social gatherings due to feeling ill because I haven't felt "myself." Yet it has transpired that I wasn't ill. I think I was just being made aware that I was not in the position to cope. Although I have often regretted missing these occasions, I do think it's important to acknowledge how you are feeling and act accordingly.

Since discovering and developing means of protection, I no longer have to absent myself from social gatherings.

If you feel vulnerable or are having to face a situation which may cause you to feel that way, there are a variety of ways by which you can shield yourself.

Certain **herbs and essences** are available for providing a shield or to remove negativity. Look on line for details of those which are beneficial, how they work and how to use them.

Some **minerals** also have beneficial properties and you'll find links to these too.

Again there are **visualisation techniques** that are useful for protection. There are two which I use, both taught to me by Rachel, who played such a great part in helping me. As with anything new, the techniques have to be practiced in order to be learned.

One is to imagine a beautiful cloak or large wrap. See it in your mind, fashion it for yourself, any shape, material, style or colour. It is yours and yours alone. Feel it wrapping around your body as you snuggle into it. Let its comfort and warmth help you to relax and feel its protection. Once you have established it in your mind you will have it forever. If you continue to practice using it you will always have it available whenever you need it.

The other thing you can visualize is a bubble; strong and transparent. Nothing harmful can penetrate it. It will always protect you. I found this most helpful in a large building which held many people. It was an emotional occasion and I knew I'd be vulnerable. Inside my bubble I found the volume of noise around me diminished and I felt calmer and safer. I had created my own private space.

Using Your Energy Wisely

This is another aspect that needs attention. The stresses of everyday life these days makes for a great deal of tension, which uses energy and leaves us depleted and vulnerable. We all need energy and it makes sense to use it wisely. This applies to everyone but is particular relevant to empaths.

There are numerous ways we waste energy. I remember during the birth of my son, I was shouting because of the pain and my doctor told me to stop. I was really surprised. Don't most women yell when their contractions are fierce? What he told me made a lot of sense: I was wasting energy which I would shortly be needing for the delivery. Wise words.

Yelling is a waste of energy unless used to alert someone. Losing your temper is another waste of energy, as is worrying.

I remember a mother at my children's primary school who always spoke in quite tones, whether addressing an individual or a group of any size. She never spoke loudly yet always commanded attention. She was a lady who used her energy wisely, not in the volume of her voice but in its expression. It can also makes people listen more closely.

Whatever the circumstances, our feelings generate energy that we can use in different ways. Remember to use your energy for positive things. Becoming more aware of yourself helps with that.

When you are feeling nervous, harness that energy as athletes, singers and actors do. They use their nervous energy to supplement their physical energy for a better performance. Letting nervousness build into worry doesn't help anyone, it just exhausts you. If it builds to the point of fear it is destructive.

When there is a problem you are bound to be concerned, so use your energy to find a solution.

Here are a few guidelines which I recommend:

Follow your **instincts**. If you are unsure of what to do as a result of your instinct, consider the worst case scenario. If you can be sure that there will be no harmful result from whatever action you are considering, then you can go ahead. But if you cannot be sure of that, do nothing. After all it's not your problem.

The **responsibility** for other people is theirs not yours. Although you may want to help, it may not be possible. Even if it is, remember that others need to develop their own strategies for coping. Always bear this in mind if you are contemplating any sort of intervention.

Don't overthink! If you find yourself in a dilemma you can tie yourself in knots doing this. (Didn't I just!) It confuses things and can make it difficult to recognise what you know instinctively and what are just your own thoughts and ideas. (Recognise that one?) You need to keep a clear head.

Believe in yourself. Self-doubt is extremely destructive. Don't give in to it. It made me think I was going crazy and upset my balance completely.

If your **health** has been compromised get **professional help**.

These recommendations have been written in the light of my experiences and discoveries!

And finally...

Your Special Gift

If you have identified yourself as an empath, you will always be one. You may not always be aware of it or may be constantly knowing. Cases will vary greatly in that respect, just as they can be different in the degree and manner in which we are effected.

You have a special gift, albeit one that comes with some disadvantages. You can take steps to counteract these and I hope the information I have given has been useful. The gift of being an empath may be developed if you wish and again you can find information on line.

The choice is yours but above all else.....

ENJOY YOUR BLESSINGS!

Printed in the United States
By Bookmasters